AF147310

FORTY POEMS FOR DYLAN THOMAS

ROGER STENNETT

The right of Roger Stennett to be identified as the Author of the Work has been asserted by him in accordance with the Copyright, Designs and Patents Act 1988.

Forty Poems for Dylan Thomas © Roger Stennett
Cover likeness of Thomas derived from the photography of Nora Summers
Edited and typeset by Will Rees
ISBN: 978-1-915439-32-1

Printed and bound in the UK by
4edge Limited, 22 Eldon Way Industrial Estate, Hockley, Essex, SS5 4AD

Published by
Candy Jar Books
Mackintosh House
136 Newport Road, Cardiff, CF24 1DJ
www.candyjarbooks.co.uk

All rights reserved. No part of this publication may be reproduced, stored in a retrieval system, or transmitted at any time or by any means, electronic, mechanical, photocopying, recording or otherwise without the prior permission of the copyright holder. This book is sold subject to the condition that it shall not by way of trade or otherwise be circulated without the publisher's prior consent in any form of binding or cover other than that in which it is published.

For my son Sam

Foreword

The story of Dylan Thomas – his precocious arrival, his rousing readings, his sad demise – has been told many ways and in many tongues. Most accounts concentrate on the last few years of his short life; in comparison, his early years have been largely neglected.

Roger Stennett takes a different approach: one unique not only in biographies of Dylan, but to my knowledge, in the forms of biography and poetry as a whole.

Forty Poems for Dylan Thomas is essentially a voyage through time in verse – sometimes pausing, often returning, but always striving to encompass the entirety of its complex, often contradictory subject. Dylan Thomas: the man who remained a boy at heart; the debauched love-cheat; the booze hound; the ardent lover; the devoted, imploring son; the starry-eyed visionary.

Interwoven with this creative, unique form of biography are reflections on Roger's own life in writing, a vocation sparked and fuelled by a childhood encounter with Dylan's verse.

Such seams are rich in their own right; moreover, they are a device by which Roger ingeniously explores that final piece of Dylan's story: his enduring stature as one of the world's best-loved writers.

Such explorations are original, stimulating, and sometimes provocative: the shadow of Thomas's influence falls long over contemporary Welsh literature: it is an inheritance as imposing as it is rich.

To understand Dylan the myth, we must first understand Dylan the artist; to understand Dylan the artist, we must first understand Dylan the man. But before anything, to understand any of them, we must understand Dylan the boy.

The scene-setting 'Memory of a Miler' begins with the fourteen-year-old Dylan winning the mile race at the Swansea Grammar School sports day, and ends with the discovery of a press cutting detailing the achievement in Dylan's wallet after his death. In many ways this portrait of Dylan the athlete anchors the entire collection: the boy of ambition limitless as his potential; the boy who fulfilled his dreams while still a teenager; the boy who never quite grew up.

> We all need magic. We all carry in hand or soft heart
> Furry rabbit's feet and four-leafed clovers,
> Locks of our beloved lover's hair in lockets
> To buoy us up when the world pushes us down.
> And so it was with him. Adulation freely offered
> Sometimes didn't matter quite as much, couldn't match
> One Swansea day when lungs grasped for air,
> And a skinny boy felt his very first kiss of victory.

This is not a book to read in one go but to dip into, to pick through: to revisit and to reflect on and to savour. Roger is his own poet, with his own style; but he shares with Dylan those qualities that continue to inspire readers around the world: a conviction in the heights that poetry can reach, and the ambition to attempt them.

To my mind, he has done so, crafting a collection that manages to be both lofty in theme and rooted in place, rich in language yet accessible in content, grounded in tradition yet refreshing in voice.

It is a fitting tribute to its subject, and there is no higher praise than that.

Geoff Haden
Restorer and Curator, Dylan Thomas' Birthplace
Chairman, Dylan Thomas Society

Preface

The real writing done, it's now time to write my preface.

Like every writer, I make up stories, in prose and poetry, to reflect the impact of the world on me, and to share tales in the hope of touching others. Deaths and entrances. Facts and fictions that unite and separate us all.

For me, childhood provides much material. Both Dylan and I have excavated our boyhoods, delving into that fertile land and surfacing with the foundations of stories and poems. The theatre is also a fertile ground. My father, Stan Stennett, was a comedian and jazz guitarist, for seventy years. Mum and I trekked with him, and latterly with my brother Ceri too, and I grew up in dressing rooms, from Ayr to Aberystwyth.

Around seven, formal education caught up with me, and later, three years in Cambridge, reading History, refined my vision and poetic voice. Poetry helped define me in the eyes of contemporaries, and later, through magazines and rooms above pubs, we would impose our verses upon one another, printing inky, slim volumes born from our innocence and experiences.

Ten interesting years followed as an arts administrator, giving away millions of pounds of public money to writers and theatres, arts centres and festivals as the seventies swung into the eighties. Then in 1978 I wrote my first stage play, which went on in the East End of London at the Half Moon.

Until 1984, when I became a full time dramatist, I ran writing and arts administration side by side, learning my craft and gradually working in larger venues, as well as starting to receive commissions for my work in theatre, radio drama, television and animation, including several plays for BBC Radio 4. I believe I am the only writer to have worked for both Sooty and the Royal Shakespeare Company! Other venues included the Bristol Old Vic, the Royal Exchange, and Nottingham Playhouse. I also found myself a visiting tutor conducting master classes in dramatic writing, in universities and drama schools including Oxford, Cambridge, Bristol and Bristol Old Vic Theatre School.

In my forty years of being a dramatist, I hardly wrote any poetry. I earned my living from dialogue. Then the world turned upside down. With the advent of the pandemic, all the theatres went dark, and radio, TV, and film work were scaled right back.

Lockdown came, and with it a single new poem. Now, as I write this, in August 2022, I have 2,500 new poems. The return to my first writing love kept me going through the darkest of times.

The idea for this collection started to grow. It is an undertaking I believe is unique. I do not know of another poet who has written a book of poems about a fellow poet in this way: not a volume addressed to a lover, who just happens to be a poet; a volume about a poet I have never met, but who has been with me throughout my life.

This collection starts when Dylan was fourteen years old, and moves through the stages of his life and work until the inevitable curtain fall. I have tried to vary my style and themes, helped by decades of appreciation of his work and knowledge of his stomping grounds, plus a period spent talking with Aeronwy, Dylan's daughter, as we conducted readings of our first slim volumes, published in 1976. Hers was entitled *Later Than Laugharne*. Mine was *Just a Matter of Time*.

I also had the pleasure of meeting Trefor, Aeronwy's husband, who, along with their daughter Hannah, does much to preserve legacies of both father and daughter.

Perhaps here is the place for some appreciation and thanks.

First, to my family, past, present and future, for everything they gave, and still do.

Then to Shaun and Will at Candy Jar. This is their first foray into poetry for adults, alongside their wide catalogue of other titles. Will Rees, as an editor, has been a model of professionalism and patience.

I'd like to thank Geoff Haden, owner of the Dylan Thomas Birthplace in Swansea, for writing an introduction. I am proud to be associated with the place where Dylan lived for twenty-one years and wrote some of his greatest work. https://dylanthomasbirthplace.com/

Appreciation also to the many hundreds of regular followers of my Facebook Page and other sites on which I post, some of whom have become real virtual friends along the journey of this book. (www.facebook.com/rogerpstennett)

Finally, much love and appreciation to Sheila, Ceri and Judith and special others I have met along my path, whose ears (and hearts) I've tried to bend with poetry.

Poetry matters.

I am a great believer that we all have stories to tell, and that we can acquire the tools to express our own tales. So many free resources are online. But beyond the pleasure of creation, and its therapeutic value, I share with Dylan a sense that dedication and commitment to poetry is a profound and mystical business, and that we should take the craft or sullen art seriously, both as a gift, and as an expression of our living.

Roger Stennett, 2022

Memory of a Miler

Twenty-five years carried, crumpled,
Precious in a succession of empty wallets.
Dylan Thomas treasured the memory
Of that day, in 1928, aged fourteen,
He won the Swansea Mile
At St Helen's sports ground.
Swansea Grammar boy, beaming with pride,
Not yet a poet. Time enough for that.

Images of Dylan range so widely,
From angelic upstart in an ugly, lovely town,
To bloated being, seeing his sad life disappear
Like the sun going down over Mumbles.
But not very often do we recall a spindly teen,
Kitted out to run and beat all contenders.
Coming first is unambiguous.
The finishing tape tells no lies.

The year that followed saw new entrances,
As poetic lines started to compete for attention.
Young athlete's feet replaced by metric ones.
A starting gun was fired, a new race begun,
Only to end, overseas, a quarter of a century away,
Crossing the finishing flat-line in a New York hospital,
No accolades bestowed. No medal or trophy given.
Just an obituary echoing round a darkened stadium.

But all the time, his hard miles disappeared,
Dylan carried proof, hidden like a tattered talisman,
That once upon a time he was an athlete,
And sometimes, in smoky pubs on lost rainy nights
In Uplands, or posh Upper East Side of Gotham City,
In his cups, or painfully sober, he would unfold
The newspaper cutting, creased with miles travelled,
And marked by the fingertips of his stubby poet's hands.

Beaming with the pride of his rose-tinted reflection
Dylan would, at least in that instant, seem to dismiss
All other achievements and endeavours.
Poetry, prose, play for voices, failing to breast the tape,
Always second place, on the heels of the miler,
A highlight that never dimmed. A gold medal memory
In a world that, over ticking time, raced by,
Turning gold to silver. Then bronze. Then black.

We all need magic. We all carry in hand or soft heart
Furry rabbit's feet and four-leafed clovers,
Locks of our beloved lover's hair in lockets
To buoy us up when the world pushes us down.
And so it was with him. Adulation freely offered
Sometimes didn't matter quite as much, couldn't match
One Swansea day when lungs grasped for air,
And a skinny boy felt his very first kiss of victory.

Home, Sweet Home

(Dylan Thomas Recalls)

And in the mornings
To come down the stairs
To where the house
Was waking up.
Waiting for me to arrive,
To make an entrance,
Bottle green shirt
And unruly hair damped down
And combed into submission.

The smell of tea and toast
Was always there waiting
And some days kippers sat,
Dead as Captain Cat's sailors.
I frowned at the order of it
And made a mental note
To trumpet my untidiness.
A poet needs a spot of manure
For ideas to grow. We all know that.

Making morning conversation
About cabbages and deposed kings
And civil war in sunny Spain
And how it's money down the drain
To rent beer in Uplands pubs,
Only to pee it down the lavatory later.

I made all the right noises,
My snout snuffling behind the paper
An ink-black shield against family intimacy.

Then, promising to be home early,
I slipped on my surly jacket
Against winter wind rising from the Bay
And started my imaginary slalom run,
Skiing down past Clevedon Court,
Then Richmond Road upon the left,
And then down along the Grove
Towards Sketty and western civilisation.
Buses, standing stationary. Steaming.

Home is where you hang your pork pie hat,
Or so the cliché goes. And I know
When I return back here tonight,
Weary from words and maybe a little tight
From my journalistic tinctures in the local,
I will time my climb back up the hill
Precise as the last few precious drags
On my self-conscious Woodbine,
And entering will announce my arrival,
Enquiring whether there's any supper
Needing me to eat it?

A Return Journey... Once More

Back here and God knows how.
More like Prospero than Dylan.
Magic manufactured a man shaped from dust,
Synthesised, and sent home to Swansea town
To see if anything's left worth caring about now.

Where to start? Naturally, the park.
Stand by the gravel-filled fountain
And the scale and size surprises.
A childhood sense of proportion.
Familiar giant places all handkerchief small.

Has that ball you threw up into the air
Made a safe landing yet? I wonder.
And where to are your small mates,
Strawberry sweet and no doubt mitching,
Sure as God made scrumped green apples?

And in your inner-eye do tiger-shadows
Still play striped tricks in balmy sunshine?
Does summer imagination perform legerdemain
As the pained hunchback waltzes with his Lady of Bones,
And all the world's a Variety stage. Or pantomime.

But it's getting late, and owls, altar-wise,
Are flying, and their hooting reminds you
Of the soon coming moon and sharp stars

Rising up out of crow black Swansea Bay.
And even Sketty boily boys need beauty sleep.

No 5 Cwmdonkin Drive
(Even the address rhymes),
The place you first saw the light
And screamed the word 'Home'.
A place where they have to take you in.

Remember all those dusky strolls
From bosky Cwmdonkin trees
Downhill, homeward, for evaporated milk
Straight from a pierced and punctured tin?
Life truly doesn't get much better. Ever.

Quiet, the old place. Neat and tidy.
Museum-bright and well organised.
No striped pyjamas draped over banisters.
Chamber pots tucked, all china ready.
PC Attila Rees could pee in peace here.

How very many times you have carried
Pints upstairs, hidden inside a bulging bladder,
Mountaineering stairs to a summit, single bed,
Flag limp. Head pounding. Oxygen starving.
Trying not to awaken others, and failing.

Finding your bed, sighing a beery prayer,
Aware you didn't bother quite to kneel,
You spend a seagull-serenaded night
Wheeling on high seas, skippering SS *Kidwelly*,
Ogling fishy bosoms of Mumbles mermaids.

Once upon (below) a time you wake
Next morning, cold reality dawning
About just who you kissed last night
Up Salubrious Passage, under cover
Of darkness, and an avalanche hangover.

Curious as any Alice's Wonderland,
The once familiar house fills up with modern strangers
Of all hues, who choose to walk right through you,
Staring at your frozen pictures on the walls
Failing to see your ghostly truth standing before them.

No time for ectoplasmic bacon and eggs.
Laugharne to visit, then on to Fern Hill,
To knit and plough furrowed brows, and try to recall
Long distant days, not always easy to picture,
Times when lilting laughter was a childhood friend.

Retracing steps, tracking yourself down,
Like pursuing some wild animal.
Following your paw marks made in muddy memory,
Determined to find that hidden hunchback dog kennel.

Turning in decreasing circles, travelling hopefully,
And then to arrive and find the past fled,
Time's five bar gate clumsily left open,
Horses long strayed across fields of song,
And people who once belonged long dead,
Ancient mariners who sailed the windfall light with you.

And though parks and precious places remain,
Curated and conserved with loving kindness,
A simple truth: our homes recede
Like mirages in hour-glass sands.
Oases retreating, always just beyond our reach.

And what is there to show for any of it?
Sepia pictures and monochromatic poems,
Staged pieces, suggesting Dylan just stepped out
To buy a beer in Uplands, or a whisky down at Brown's.
His chair still warm. His bombazine voice still echoing.

And we will wait, quiet and patient, like acolytes,
For the sound of a skeleton's key turning
In the lock of memory, and the creak
Of a once familiar front door
That sings to us, in booming baritone,
Of a return journey, once more.

Deep. Dark. And Fathomless

An old picture postcard,
Maybe the day of my arrival.
The Wenallt, around 1960.
Arriving as a ten year child
To live on Rhiwbina Hill,
Thrilled to be there,
Marvelling over open spaces
And across the shallow valley
Where Cwm Norfydd trickled.
The grassy Wenallt Mountain,
Site of childhood games
Yet to be fought and won,
On fern-carpeted slopes,
Amidst trees as young as forever,
Which today envelop
All the child-friendly hillsides.

A little like Dylan's Fernhill,
Happy as the grass was green,
Young and easy in the mercy of time,
Which back then was never mean
Or niggardly, but stretched out serenely
All the long days, long, to gentle dusk
And foxes running, and the coming
Out of night stars I recognised
From Brooke Bond tea cards
Glued inside my cherished album.

And each evening to say the words
'Good night' to bracken and to trees
And to steep paths where I skinned my knees,
Proving a good time had been had.
A place to play where I could stray safely,
Soundly as the Cardiff sunset set
Behind the hill. Behind our house.

Craig-y-Nos. House built on a hill.
Rock of the Night.
Cotswold stone hand-carved
By Venetian stone masons
Travelling to work not by gondola
But No.21 bus, Pantmawr Junction stop.
In health and in sickness we lived there,
From Swinging Sixties through Millennium,
Until at a stroke, the slow drawing down of blinds.

It was true home wherever else was
Or might have been, temporarily. True rock.
Grounded. A strong place and a beacon.
Safe in floods. Cosy in blasts of snow,
Which dad and Ceri and freezing me dug out,
To clear the car way to pantomime performances.
The true cliché that the show always must go on.
From this place eventually I sailed away,
As children do and must, and I trusted
The universe to guide me, my tea-card stars

To point the way. A Polaris pole star shining
To set my sextant, and it was waves of words
That washed me outwards, helped me fledge,
Become the Albatross cuckoo in the nest,
Crosscurrents and tidal current rips
That stole me from my safe and sleepy shore
And more and more take my ship to sea,
Like the Argo of Greek mythology,
Driving me to seek and try to find
Beyond the Pillars of Hercules,
Off on my own Odyssey to discover
The blessed Fair Isles of my own mystery,
Childhood's dreams and widening horizon,
Overflowing into the wild, wide sea.

And we all set sail. Some tumbled from Mumbles
And doggy-paddled, heads barely above water.
Some simply no better than they should be,
Breast stroked like it was going out of style,
Or pinned school medals on puffed up chests
And did the crawl for all to see and admire.
Jump in, or be thrown, into the deep end,
Getting bearings in herring-bullied waves,
Before striking out along the golden pathway
Of rising, then setting sun, painted on the water,
To find an end to their beginning
And begin to find a way to an ending.
Sad, salty eulogies, sung by seagulls,

Over Swansea Bay, or downtown Manhattan.
Mumbled in all our hopeful prayers as we plunged
Like Byron to swim our own Hellespont.

And we really all tried our very best
To swim, or surf, the sea of riptide words,
And sometimes we would fail, nobly,
And almost drown in faraway deep waters.
Like Dylan T in NYC, a city that never sleeps.
The great white way. No beacon. No sailors warning.
But a razzle-dazzling beckoning of Scylla and Charybdis,
Whores' bloodshot eyes served on the rocks and reefs
That lie beneath Gotham streets, to do their very worst.
Finally they bleached his fragile bones as coral white
As Blind Captain Cat and all his Taffy shipmates,
Who sailed as human ballast away from Milk Wood
With a cargo of true Welsh lies, and bitter surprises,
To try to trade across seven oceans, wide and deep,
Fated never to make safe home again, to port,
Apart from in these sea shanty lines of mine,
And Dylan's words. Deep. Dark. And fathomless.

As Flies To Wanton Boys

Praise God
We are a poetic nation,
To steal and half-inch
And alter a Dylan line.
But it's true. Praise whatever
God might be, today, in this
Our multi-faith place.
Not many faces of different hues
Lived in Milk Wood. Maybe you noticed?
Though I never did, until the moment
I wrote that line. But that's fine,
For I fond and foolishly attest
The artist known as Dylan T
Sang what he saw. Perfect imperfect lives.
Broken Biscuits that still tasted lush.

Just as he saw, sometimes
Through a pint glass, darkly, but honestly,
With just a few useful extra fibs scattered
Like sixpences in a Christmas pud
That a young dog might well have nibbled.
A poet is made of many parts.
At heart a common man,
Common as the next one.
Common as the common cold.
Common as, well, just common, see.
But maybe he, or she, has bits

Overdeveloped. Empathy for starters.
Heartfelt ability to meld and mould
Him or her into others' minds, kindly purloining
Anything found, and in a green way
Make do and mend, to fashion poetry.

All a bit Blue Peter but sadly without
Sticky-back adhesive and squeezy bottles.
A good eye comes next, to see what others miss,
Even when pissed, and to take a note
Of which pub you're in, and whether the landlord
Will ban you for collapsing, and showering
In the urinal-spitting Gents. God help,
And it makes no sense at all,
If you haven't got an ear to hear
How real words sound, tumbling from
Mouths of mumbling Mumbles men,
And cockle-women with mermaid-tales to tell.

And then it helps to have a voice to declaim
And a nose to sniff out themes and dreamily
Filch other men's wives, and just as shocking,
Steal other men's shirts, whilst transatlantic
Promenading and pillaging,
Using sharp poems as blunt weapons,
Grievous bodily rhyme. A word crime
As sure as God made little green apples
For scrumping Swansea kids to munch

On merry Mumbles mitching days
From picture perfect grammar school.
And finally it helps to have a subject.
Me. A word weaver too, in the same
Craft and sullen arts-man ship as him,
How many times have I've smiled
When challenged with the innocent inanity,
'Where do you get your ideas?'
And I long to reply, 'Why, I buy them by the box
Down the Co-op. Dividend stamps included.'

So in essence that's the quintessential
Quintessence of it. Kind of an Airfix kit
Of how poets are made and stuck together,
Never forgetting ham-fisted splodges
Of glue in easy, pin-pricked metal tubes
On long wet winter afternoons
In the Principality, in the 1950s.
I learnt joined up writing in sleepy Cardiff
Just as Dylan T was falling apart. Eyes wide open,
Oceans apart, but like all writers joined somehow.

Till one day we separate to lead rhyme times
Of our own. New voices. Separate tongues, forking
But forever bearing a port wine-stain birthmark,
Undisguised and forever recognisable pain.
Cut from the same cloth
Fashioned into individual disguises,

Tumbling and tripping over words
That say everything, and yet nothing too,
In a land that pays lip service to its bards
But at the same time, really doesn't.
As another said, those damned deities
Treat us shamefully.

'As flies to wanton boys are we
 To the gods, they kill us for their sport.'

Park Water under the Bridge

Spillway takes away
Overflowing water
From Roath Park Lake.
Down man-made steps,
It treads away yesterdays,
Each cascading drop carrying
Memories of once felt joy
Far away downstream,
To make the winding journey,
First to river, then on to sea,
Tumbling into Cardiff Bay
On the way to find final freedom,
And tell our tales to the tides.

My generation passed this way,
A shower of 1950s water drops,
Innocent as Dylan's strawberry boys.
We came in antique pushchairs,
Or sitting on grandad's wheelchair,
Squabbling with my cousin, over place
And petulant pecking order.
Like the visiting water birds
In Dylan's very own Cwmdonkin,
We settled early upon our playground.
And then to awake the ferns and flowers
And make the tossed and turned rose-beds,
We trod mysterious bowers that invited you
To take tea inside with all your friends.

Dylan and me, we shared many magic lands.
Later, and many miles and decades apart
(But always there in heart and fond memory),
We recalled where a story lived behind each tree,
Well thumbed encyclopaedias of adventures
In which to dip our toes, as a remembrance,
As time and life flowed over the lake's lip
And slipped away, spilt, like a tipped pint glass.
A park is a universe fenced behind iron railings,
A place that leaves a glorious, indelible mark,
Long after the hunchback is chained away,
After the park keeper exiles us at day's end.
But gaps always exist in memory's railings.

Once again, I've done it. Unexpectedly
Written another poem with Dylan
In short trousers, playing in boyhood
Along with me, a sometimes lonely only child,
Back in the days of riding on my bampa's wheelchair
As he, marooned by a stroke, was castaway
On Roath Park's island, dreaming his adventures
Of visiting here as a boy himself. And so it goes.
Endless generations tumble down the slipway.
And in my own allocation of lifetime
I've brought here first my son, then his children,
To feed the greedy ducks, and to slip on the slide,
Under a sun that is only young once.

Dark Golden Hour

Each morning, whilst darkness
Still covers me, like a duvet,
I awake, roused from sleep
By head, heart or bladder
(Take your pick)
And open up my eyes
To the familiar surprise
Of another predictable day,
Darkly waiting to amaze me.

The Golden Hour:
A term movie makers use,
The time towards day's end
When fading golden sunlight
Is still bright enough to flatter,
Though actors are well aware
Night is creeping in, inevitably.
But in this special time of late luminance,
Stars still try to shine before real stars appear.

I have my opposite situation.
An hour or sometimes more
Before the sun rises for the day,
Before morning glory
Hardens and makes its effect,
In that time of darkest darkness,
Before brand new dawn I write,
Not longhand words on spindrift pages
But pixels upon an iPad screen.

Silence is my silent witness
Until I call for music in the dark,
And automatically sound appears
For my ears only, as a smart speaker
With a woman's name obeys
My gentle call for soft tunes,
And matching my imploring whisper
Plays back my desires pianissimo
Into my sleep-dust filled ears.

Accompanied by sweet music
Flowing from so many hands and brains,
I celebrate the tuneful gifts I receive,
And tap out words baptised in blackness.
Do I believe? Do I get a dark amen? Oh yes.
And here I try to coincide with greatness,
And pause from writing to run and find
Collected Poems 1934-52. Dylan Thomas
Sitting, patient, squashed upon my bookshelf.

Respectfully, I quote,
'In my craft or sullen art
Exercised in the still of night
I labour by singing light
Not for ambition or bread
Or the strut and trade of charms
On the Ivory stages.' Not me neither.
I too write for lovers who simply do not care.

So, my own sun still hiding in the east,
I find a feast of words to pick and mix
Then serve them up to all the hidden faces
Behind the green lights that glow
On distant Internet sites, waking.
Is it, I wonder, too early to intrude?
Is it rude to chance an awakening?
Before my brain objects I press send.
They needed a wake up call anyway!

The dark before the dawn. Cliché's place
Of calamities. That's my chosen field of play.
The battle site where I marshal an army
Of words. Metaphors. Similes. Assonances
To assault senses. To make yet more rhymes
For these virally sick times in which we're living.
Lines to mount Pope's rocking horse of rhyme
And we're off, galloping across the fields of time.

Jumpers for Goalposts

Jumpers for goalposts,
As young boys that was the rule
When Dylan came to play with me
On Whitchurch Common
In the Cardiff sunshine.
Far from Cwmdonkin Park,
But on my little patch of Eden,
No chained cup fountain,
And even with an Ararat chapel,
No biblical mountain either,
Just a flat grass nothingness
With a squeaky metal roundabout
Getting me, giddily, nowhere fast.

Dylan was a slip of a lad back then,
Fast as a whippet in black daps,
Winner of his Grammar School Mile.
He carried the newspaper cutting
In his wallet to the grave,
Saving it to show to God
To prove he wasn't always
What time and tell-tales made.
Seven stone soaking wet,
An Artful Dodger playing with me,
Jolly Roger, skinnier still.

We played all the expected childhood games.
Hide and Seek, British Bulldog with butties,

Subbuteo table football down on the floor,
Falling to our knees to flick around
Cardboard and plastic soccer heroes,
Careful not to lean on them. And I showed
Him my botched and gluey masterpieces
Of Airfix aeroplanes, propellers stuck firm
Like hands upon Rupert Brooke's church clock
In Grantchester. Paused endlessly
At honey tea time. Ten to three time.

But our favourite game of all
Was played with an old leather ball.
Jumpers for Goalposts,
When all the poets came to play.
We'd pick up sides, choosing carefully
From serried ranks of versifiers.
Who'd be best goalie? Who best in midfield?
Who was out to lunch, dreaming of daffodils
Growing in profusion along the wing?

Club-footed Byron was a great full back,
Solid as a brick shithouse, a future
Nobby Stiles, but with teeth and smiles.
Wordsworth was hard work, in fairness.
'Xander' Pope spiteful, twisted and bitter,
But a better inside left you'll never find,
Playing rocking horse jinking rhyme games
Around forwards, wasp of Twickenham, stinging.

The foreign lads seemed very cocky.
Baudelaire was very rarely there,
And Arthur Rimbaud brought liquorice
That would give us all the runs. But such fun!
Goethe, in between the sticks,
Was a Teutonic given, a safe pair of hands.
Blind Johnny Milton was referee.
We all felt childishly sorry for him
And loved his confused guide dog,
Paradise Lost. And yes. He was.

And look, on the invisible touchline,
Shakespeare sits, observing all.
Some said he was a scout
For struggling Stratford United,
Some thought his scratchy quill
Wrote (almost) thrilling match reports
For the *Echo*. Some simply wondered
Why he never ever joined in.
Gay days, golden days,
Birth of rock and roll days.
Grazing knees and getting stitches,
Magic sponge and bumpy pitches
Maybe not the playing fields of Eton.
We all ate our fill of half time treats,
Black Jacks, Fruit Salads and packs
Of soft candy cigarettes. There's wicked.

Out of puff and out of time
We rhymers still bemoaned

The shrill final whistle
Sending everyone homeward bound,
To far shires and blue remembered hills,
Back to gas-filled killing fields of Passchendaele
Or amorous deeps where Shelley died,
Or to Asylum with Gloucestershire Ivor Gurney,
Or maybe like the fibber Tommy Chatterton
(Lying through his pretty Bristol City teeth)
Dead in a Holborn attic, mouth full of arsenic.
But whatever befell them, for a fine time
We all were friends, as only boys can be.

Dylan always had to go, saying cheerio
Around five, to catch the smoky, puffing
Chuffing train to Swansea Jack town.
(Still not yet a proper city. Poor dabs.)
We'd swap Brooke Bond tea cards
And slurped dark glasses of dandelion & burdock
Making mad promises we could never keep
Of regular letters and pen-friend chatter,
Both knowing that, faster than a free kick
Swiftly taken, we and all the away team
Would be up to something new,
Faster than you could say
'Lava Bread and salty cockles'
Washed down by fizzy Corona pop,
Down through windfall rivers
Of our kind and still open minds.

Maybe, in Time, Time Itself Will Tell

In my poetic imagination
I am the unseen one,
The all seeing private eye
Who invisibly walks besides,
As poets capture butterflies
Or press flowers into a memory book.

I look and see what they do,
A half-heartbeat behind,
But close enough to feel
The sunshine of creation,
The anvil hammer heat
As words are struck and folded.

Marvel over the alchemy
Of poetic transmutation,
Forged within the cauldron,
Magicians practising legerdemain,
Pulling rhyming rabbits out of hats,
Awaiting the arrival of gold, glistening.

I walked with Dylan in Cwmdonkin,
Larking about. Just two young kids
Happy as mochyns in cachu,
As two imaginary friends
We sailed our boats
In the gravel-bottomed fountain.

And my eyes were illuminated
By sunshine yellow of daffodils
As high on lakeside hills and dales
William and I wandered,
Never lonely, though floating
Blown on summer breezes.

Head down I slogged through mud
And blood, trickling like mountain streams
As with Shropshire Wilfred we tried to rhyme
While all the time aware of whizz bangs
Bursting above our heads, strewing shrapnel
On poor bloody Tommy Atkins down below.

And Samuel and me, we strongly advised
The Ancient Mariner not to try to shoot
The Albatross that soared above the mast,
But eyes blinded by thirst, he slew the bird
And was forever cursed, doomed never to forget,
Thirst never slaked. Bird blood clotting in his throat.

And many more poetic places I have been,
And keenly seen visions that other poets saw,
Then spun into garments of wonderment.
I charged the guns with the Light Brigade,
Stopped one Oxfordshire summer day at Adlestrop,
And sat with sad Oscar as his cell door slammed shut.

Bluebird of happiness? Or squawking parrot,
Sitting unseen on shoulders of poetic giants,
Trying to peek further, beak chattering,
To spy the long lineage of the line,
The heredity of harmonies of words,
The ancestry of those who went before.

There were, of course, other times
I walked and rhymed with rhymers,
Watched oiled cogs of fine minds turning
And heard the tick-tock of chiming clocks
Rhyming and ticking to count the hours
For decades. Or a few short moments more.

One final question, one enigmatic puzzle,
For as I've strolled through literary labyrinths,
Far from ever reaching their amazing centres,
I've felt my own presence shadowed
One foot, one stanza behind me. Who could it be?
Maybe, in time, time itself will tell.

Looking for the Sweet Trolley

I wonder if Dylan had been here
In these two-Facebook times,
Trying to rhyme and circulate poetry,
I wonder what his fate would be,
In an age of online trolls and bedsitter Byrons
Eager to trash craftsmanship as passé
And drafts simply as chilly winds, blowing.

Upstairs in Sketty, no pettifogging
From the man of handwritten letters,
The boy who graduated from the park
And from his windows spied the baying sea
And sang songs to it, and shared dreams,
Friends with mumbling waves, on spindrift pages,
Old exercise books bursting with sweaty testosterone.

Writing, and rewriting the rewriting of it all,
Methodical and neatly arranged,
Peppered with second thoughts and third
Absurd amendments. Lines crossed out
With school ruler precision, new ones inserted
Bottle green colour, shirted Rimbaud
Of number 5 Cwmdonkin Drive.

How different would it be now?
He'd simply tap a button,
To reveal a grubby window on the world,

Bigger than anything he could ever see
From his ordered single bedroom,
Sash glass window pane,
Where Swansea Jack watched rain rap.

Tapping keypad and pressing send
His poems would wend their way,
Cast a girdle around the world
In less time than typing cat and mat,
Slide into a billion inboxes,
Always open to receive outpourings
Manufactured by the new marvellous boy.

Hard to know whether he'd have survived
The slings and arrows of outrageous trolls
Whose reason for living seems to be
Discouraging well-constructed poetry,
Preferring their own incontinent angst,
Projectile free verse, regurgitated similes,
All the freshness of last night's Biryani.

But had he been cyber-connected,
What then? No need to travel overseas
For poetry reading, shirt stealing
And transatlantic dalliances,
For slow, slippery, carnal dances.
Far easier on body and mind,
Far more kind to seek approval
From faceless Facebook likes.

History would need to be rewritten,
A counter-factual chapter penned.
Dylan would not end on a New York slab,
But cold feet secure in tartan slippers,
He'd shuffle round the Boat House,
Wi-Fi equipped, fibre modem roasting hot,
Broadbanding everything he'd got.

A different world, different times
And places. Tracing his merry way
Across the grizzled face of poetry
Preserved on Facebook's curated places,
Where poetic impropriety has no space
And everything creatively luscious and lascivious
Is censored by tiny minds, how he'd hate it.

On second thought, we'd rather leave you
As you were. Post First World War,
Growing in the mercy of time's means
And skinning knobbly knees in the park,
Scrumping apples, snowballing fires,
Stealing kisses, mitching from school,
Being an innocent, strawberry boily boy.

Dylan, you are too good for these sad days.
Let's praise you as a long dead poet of worth,
Since now we live in a very different society,
Which soon will have you safely filed away
With Byron, Browning and footsore Bunyan,
Uncomfortable with your God-given gifts.

Where Dylan grafted, modern poets grift.
Once, upon a poetry tour, in Gloucestershire,
I sat and spoke and ate food with Aeronwy,
And that night we tried to put the world to rights
And failed, of course, in loving cups of laughter.
Dylan's only daughter, and me a comedian's son,
While Dylan's hungry ghost lurked behind our backs
Looking for the sweet trolley.

A Mystery That's Ours

I've got a bone to pick
With you, Dylan T,
Not just for me
But for generations
Of Welsh writers
Who have slaved away,
Not down the pit
But penning poems
For literary journals
And force feeding
Anorexic volumes,
Puffing up their cheeks
To try to stand alongside you,
And failing miserably.

Though you've been dead
Almost seventy years
You do not go gentle
And so have become a hazard
Upon the poetic highway,
Both lanes blocked
By metaphorical roadkill
Refusing to budge an inch
Even though you are well dead,
Buried and thoroughly decomposed.

It's not your fault that you were good,
Truth be told, far better than that.
Nothing really prepared you
For the bardic crown to slip
And take up permanent resting space,
Askew above your pugnacious eyebrows.
You've got to learn to share, mun.
There's poets tamping mad out there,
Breathing fire like apprentice dragons,
Never able to set the world ablaze
While your reputation smoulders,
Still far too hot to handle.

Don't worry, Dylan,
There'll be no fisticuffs
No hold my jacket moment,
Or macho step outside fandango.
No, Dylan, all we young bloods
Have grown up, grown older,
Sensitive plants, lifetimes stunted
In your shade and brittle-boned shadow.
And as we approach and try to ride
Our own white horse of the heart
We just shyly squeeze around you,
Starved of sustenance by your bulk,
Longing for our expected moments
In the sun, our fifteen minutes of fame.

But we will forgive you. Most people did,
And as a runner up prize we'll be content
With serried ranks of silvers and bronzes.
As on the drink-puddled public bar
There you are. Your dazzling poetic gold
Glittering and outshining all the others,
Even though it floats in warm spilt beer.
We cheer you and your childhood stories.
No sign of 'Road Clear' anytime soon.
Welsh writers, all misshapen, simply learned
To live beneath your whisky shot glass ceiling,
Ascending within reason, as we love and hate you
And hold you in our hearts, a mystery that's ours.

Miracles

Waking, I call out for Johann Sebastian Bach,
And as if by serendipitous magic, music happens.
Cello. Piano. Organ. 'Sheep May Safely Graze'
Or 'Jesus, Joy of Man's Desiring' join me.
Notes and floating harmonies straighten out
My night-tossed duvet cover, and smother me
With arpeggios, kind and benignly engaging
In a pillow fight of duck down feathers flying.

And I am reminded, in the dawning of a new day,
Of Reverend Eli Jenkins, praying for safe passage
Of the town, across the dark waves of the night,
To survive and see another daylight peep
From the mystic east, destined to disappear
Over Sir John's Hill at close of day, when foxes play
And silhouettes of nightmare horses gallop.
But this is not Milk Wood. Not even semi-skimmed.

'Bach fach,' Eli breathed out from his milk stoutness,
While down the street Organ Morgan manipulated.
Stops were unstopped and foot pedals trodden
And treadled, like a kitten coaxing at the nipple,
And it's 'Organ, organ, all the time' with him,
His long suffering, skin and bone wife attests,
And string vests do not encourage great passion,
As they trawl and haul hairy chests to landfall.

Meanwhile my little smart speaker falls silent,
As if to testify that too much beauty
Can turn even high-tech machines mute,
Just as too much conducting in the dreaming dark
Can cause the spark to disappear,
And turn all of us into no good boyos
Sightless in Gaza, blind like Samson Agonistes,
No use at all. Only here to make the pillars fall.

We live in a world waiting for the other shoe
To drop. We've all seen and felt and suffered
Things lately we never thought we'd spy
Through eyes we believed had seen it all.
And to me too, who first saw the light
In the dog days of 1940s Cardiff,
These seem the end of days. Even Eli,
In his windy chapel, surely would agree.
And Dylan, he just about managed to see
The second Elizabethan age come in June,
But didn't hang about long after that,
To feel the nation's honeymoon of hope,
Though in July, Llangollen Eisteddfod
Caused him to sigh in Celtic satisfaction.

A little notebook filled with pencil scribble
Records our Welsh nation innocently at play,
Sharing wholesome sunny July days

With all the colours of a Yugoslav rainbow.
Steel helmeted Javanese, and look there,
Three Ukrainians, performers, not sad refugees,
And in an enigmatic, unfinished sentence of yours,
'The best thing that's happened in Wales since...'

The rest is silence, and soon silence swallowed him
And his singing voice. His bright chapel consonants,
His mellow, mellifluous tone, now only to be found
Going round and round on boxed black vinyl.
And still it does, or through Internet technology
Springs up, as obediently as Alexa bringing me
My early morning cup of crow-black Bach tea
And repentant charcoal biscuit to start my sinful day.

Yesterday the Queen was born, ninety-six years before,
And pictures of her, looking frail but just about here
Flicker on TV, between the images of Ukrainians
Not dancing but dying, and most certainly not
Going gentle into that good night.
Soon she will be gone as well, HRH the Queen.
The Elizabethan Era, against which my life has been lived,
Will disappear, and with it many old certainties.

But Dylan disappeared before the movie started.
He didn't hang around to view the coming glories
Or stay, popcorn in hand, to see the flickering acetate
Pass through the cinema projector's gate

And turn from monochrome to blowsy technicolour,
Clattering on to cool autumn, and soon winter is coming.
The old Queen soon will die. Delusional to think otherwise,
And we will walk forward, eyes cast back over our shoulders.

Are you surprised that people still can dance and sing
in a world on its head? The only surprising thing about miracles
however small, is that they sometimes happen.

Dylan Thomas

Never to Sail Back Home Again

Park.
Night.
Sleeping
Chained
Hunchback
Deeply
Snoring
Alleluias.
Nocturnal
Tall
Tales
Wagging
Regular
As
Any
Lord.
Cut
Glass
Clock
Chiming.
Eyes
Half
Closed
Dreaming
Goodbyes.
Midnight
Arriving.

His
Stroked
Dog-ears
Hear
Stained
Glass
Slippers
Shattering
As
She
Runs
From
The
Threat
Of
Sketty
Sunrise
Washing
Over
Swansea
Bay.
Pantomime
Tides
Mumbling,
Making
Mumbles
Promises.

Wasted
Wanton
Words,
Hearts
Broken
Before
They
Fall
On
Deaf
Gravel
Ears
In
The
Fountain
Basin
Where
A
Young
Boy
Sailed
His
Ship
Across
The
Ocean,
Destined
One

Day
To
Go,
Never
To
Sail
Back
Home
Again.

Nos Da

Bombs tumble from the bellies
Of fat Heinkels and slim Dorniers
Flying high across Swansea skies,
Fumbling the black landscape
To paint the town red with fire.

'An ugly, lovely town,' Dylan said.
Now the Luftwaffe's flying pencils
Edit and clear the way for revisions,
Second drafts. Like your notebooks,
Like your poems, but with bodies buried.

You were not there, that night of nights.
In London, you were, dancing to your own rhythm
As Teutonic ordnance tumbled from above,
But love and fond memory for your childhood place
Must have shone, incendiary, from your face.

All my poetic life I've seen you,
As many once-young poets do,
Walking, invisibly, by my side,
Full of unstoppable shaggy dog stories
Of former glories, sketty sing-songs.

Me, a Cardiff boy, allegedly sworn enemy
Of all and any Swansea Jacks. But no.
Welsh blood flows, or flowed, in both our veins,
A little past its sell by date, it's true, but you and me
Bleed as dragon-red as any under these ruins.

In years to come, the bulldozers came
And wrote brand new Swansea Sonnets
Without the help of you or me.
Some odes have stood time's test,
Others are best forgotten, or recycled.

My dear dad, Stan, played Swansea Empire
When the 1950s was still young. Pantomime
In the shadow of still unfilled bomb sites,
Trying to create some childish laughter
In a world where adults, sadly, failed.

Roll on the grandfather clock
To the 1970s, and HTV
Commissioning a poem from me,
'Dylan and me, we never spoke Welsh',
A telling line that I remember.

Haven't seen you for a while, mind.
Lonely it's been, walking on my own.
You've mitched off to a leafy early grave,
Leaving the rest of us to save the world
With pop-gun poems and stunned blank verses.

Aeronwy, your sweet and lookalike daughter,
Ate at my table and slept under my roof,
And sometimes deep in her ouija eyes
I looked for you, and for some proof
I'd walked the right road. None came.

But sometimes, at night, as I wait for sleep to come
Un-punctually you slipper in, full of beery excuses,
I hear you settle down in your hunchbacked kennel
And dog-whisper into my ear, 'Nos Da.'
And both of us know just what it means.

Sullen Dead Poets Society

Like all of us, Dylan
Got some things right,
And others very wrong.
It's not my place
To be judge or jury
Of a lifetime spent searching
For a quiet churchyard
And a simple grave.

He was, though, a man
Fond of well-turned phrases,
Spinning words like wood
Upon a lathe, and like a carpenter
Producing beauty and utility,
Precision in verse and story
To stand in stark relief
To a life lived with chaos his best friend.

But when he spoke of poetry
He was incisive and crystal clear.
Far more than just an artisan,
He shaped and polished words
To within a shining inch
Of their metaphor-filled lives.
Serenading similes,
Romancing rhymes.

Poetry was not for him
A verbal quickie
Up Salubrious Passage
In old Swansea town,
But sweat of the brow
Caught inside a bottle.
Application to screaming point.
Dreaming perhaps, and then scheming
Of how to mount poetic butterflies
Without killing jar, or sticking pin showing.

'In my craft and sullen art',
That's what he wrote,
Emphasising the manual approach,
Word shavings of discarded letters
Planed down and falling from his desk,
Gathering in a curling snow of unused feeling
Around his toes, toenails always
Twinkling with mischief.

Second, 'sullen'. Unfortunate
But true. Poets often see beer
Or whisky glass half-empty
Or fully drained. Dylan did.
And as his life attests,
When better things to do
Came along, he did them
Often with sweet relief.

No one asks to become a poet.
Why, for God's sake, would they?
The pay's not great, for a start
And hand on heart, the hours stink,
As your Muse arouses you,
Night on night, a demon succubus,
Not for consensual feats of passion,
But to take down her dictation

And ultimately, to what end?
So you can try to pay the gas bill
With a Petrarchan sonnet, and guilty smile.
The industry of exploitation is everywhere.
Ted Hughes once told me, over drinks,
He no longer signed his books
Because, before the ink was dry,
They were upon the marketplace.

'Sullen' seems to be on the money.
Unborn generations of parasitic scholars
Will grow fat, feasting off sullen poets
Dead and decaying, giving cryptic readings
To deaf and earless earth worms
Who have no taste for blank cheque verse,
Just hunger for sullen poets, themselves.

The Circus Animals' Departure

They were here again last night,
The actors of my dream team,
Strolling players, performers,
Thespians of un-woke times,
Unwashed but not unwanted,
Lounging around inside my head.
Spaced out, some of them,
As some actors may be,
Living lives of uncertainty,
Playing cast off parts, chasing crumbs
Like frenzied truffle-hounds,
Benign but biding time
Rehearsing rhymes and rhythms,
Entrances and exits, lines and cues,
Written by writers just like me.

In my sweet dream I was offering tea
At an audition for my latest play,
While they all posed and postured
With polished, practised nonchalance,
As if to say, 'I really don't need the part,'
While on their fraying sleeves
Their dear lying hearts were bleeding,
Pleading for me to give them a chance,
To dance with my left-footed words
And try, as Noel Coward recommended,
Simply to 'get on', speak and to exit
Without knocking over the furniture.

And here they were,
Innocent as raspberries,
A phrase made by a Swansea Jack
Who some time back
Also herded actor cats.
For that is how it feels,
Even in an immortal Play for Voices.
Aren't they all? Plays are not dumbshows
Performed my mumbling Mumbles mummers
But let that curious description stand.

Seventy years ago, an outcrop in literary history,
These actors are now mine to motivate
Above or below a time. In the Beginning
And in my Ending. And all points in between.
Clad in bible-black bombazine of my dreaming
Or lately fled, like nightmares in the hayrick fields
Of Fern Hill, galloping out of sight of light,
As sunlight dawned and morning dissolved them.

Even now as I try to set down memories
Those memories are already fading,
Forgetting their lines, without cue or clue,
As memories always do and maybe must,
To leave room for others to arrive,
Insubstantial phantoms through seven ages
Leaving not a wrack behind,
As I surface from deep sleep

In my wrecked bed of dreaming,
And vainly try to hold will-o'-wisps
Whispering between clumsy fingers
And I record the memory of a memory,
Pointless as kids snowballing a conflagration
Thanking the Lord that we are a poetic nation,
Scribbling congregants of the Reverend Eli,
As I stand and sing my own hymns,
One of a long line of Welsh rhymers,
Dreamers and pantomime comedians,
Who love to do our very best,
All the better to have children roaring
From dark, sweet wrapper-littered stalls.

Time for tea. Predictably I've rambled and ambled,
And in that once upon a time they've all gone.
Disappeared. Resting. Doing very odd jobs,
Till all theatres open again, including spectral ones.
They can all appear in someone else's sleeping head,
And perform, for the quick and for the dead.
My actors of Dream Time,
Aboriginals, first nations,
Indigenous itinerants
Waving faded Equity cards
And swapping Thespian tales,
They are there within our heads
To teach us something,
To hold up a mirror to human nature,

But sadly, sleeping, we don't see
Nuances and subtleties
Through sleepy-dust encrusted eyes.

And with sunrise the spotlight dies,
The longed-for limelight fades,
And one more every day begins,
The raggle-taggle troupe departs,
Blowing me insincere air kisses,
Promising to return one night soon
In the pale and moonlit glow
Of my midsummer dreaming,
To put on a show the like of which
I've never seen. And best of all
I will be its progenitor and ring master,
As circus animals sing for their supper.

And once more I will awake, suddenly,
Frustrated again at not reaching the finale,
Or being lovingly struck by the benign punch line,
Left wondering, mumbling and rhyming
At no tag line in the rag and bone shop of my heart,
Trying to puzzle out why they are all still arriving
In my crumpled bed, good theatrical digs to them,
As they posture, preen, prod, poke and joke,
Then disappear leaving their bill, still, unpaid.

We Talked of Fathers

A magic faraway look, Aeronwy,
You still had it around your eyes
When we met in Bristol
Both side-stepping into the light,
Publishing our slim volumes.
Later Than Laugharne was yours.
Just a Matter of Time was mine.
Published by the same small press
High in the hills of wild West Wales.

You stayed here. We shared poetry readings.
You dreamed dreams in our spare bed,
And we talked of fathers, yours and mine.
Ethereal, female, you, but the image.
Me too. Chip off the old comic's block.
Genes are very hard wearing, as we know.
Bits and pieces, odds and sods,
Exchanged like school kids swapping cards.

How strange, we both agreed, that nowadays
You lived in safe suburban south London,
Far away from Laugharne and its strange legacy.
You sang your chorister husband's praises
And spoke of Zen wandering in San Francisco.
Buddhism taught you stories by which to live,
And I marvelled at your Italian tongue,
As well as appreciating your poetic one.

No more than when it spoke of childhood's tales,
As mine did, theatres and old backstages my backdrop.
And your final poem, 'My Son, My Sage',
Seemed to turn life's wheel full circle,
Though reading your proud motherly lines
More than forty long years after,
I wonder what the now grown man makes
Of poetic meditations on his potty training.

A few years later
I too became a dad.
Now I'm a grandad,
Touched by dharma, too.
And I often wonder
At life's karma
And smile, Aeronwy,
When I remember you.

No Leftover Lives to Kill

No leftover lives
To kill. All gone now.
Two generations
Cards played out,
Placed upon life's table,
Folded, chips cashed.

Yet somewhere within young blood
Corpuscles course through living veins.
Something of Dylan still remains.
If life was a publishing house,
A new print run. Second editions.

Aeronwy, we talked of our fathers,
But talked of mothers too. A little.
On a night of convivial conversation
You spoke of yours, in faraway Italy,
Of Vespa scooters, and her lust for life.

One of a trio, two brothers and little you,
All gone. Trailing along rivers of windfall light
To who knows where? A country heaven
Ticked by stars, ticking? Who can say?
Aeronwy, when we sat cross-legged together
You were a Buddhist, so no Heaven necessary.

Reincarnation? A transcendent thought.
Where on earth has karma driven you?
From tortured Samsara on through Bardo,
Then finally where did you emerge?
From which rabbit hole did you spring forth
One moonlight night, high up on Sir John's Hill?

Rosie Probert

'A woman who can't say no.
Even to midgets,' Dylan wrote.
And why ever not! God help.
We all love Rosie, all the more
For her sexual inclusivity,
Though these poor, amorous midgets
Might need to try quite hard to climb
Her laddered stockings, and higher.
Their noses bleed from altitude,
But determined to show the world,
And Miss Rosie, that big things
Sometime do come in small parcels,
They do indeed. Honest to God.

She's a good sport, though which game
Is debatable. Certainly no rugger bugger,
Or muddy madam, playing an offside trap,
Nor virgin of the off-white tennis type
Beloved of dear old John Betjeman.
And good for her, that's what I say.
No Home Counties hesitation.
I'd lay a bet Rosie knows her station
And all the daffodil embankments
Down our branch line track.
I look for her in the Dingle, starry,
And far and wide on Donkey Down,
Over Sir John Hill, and left hand down
To grasp a memento mori moment.

Disgracefully beautiful, and handsome
Despite time's killer avalanches
That would have swept lesser women away,
Or encased them in a glacial trousseau.
Such a waste if sweet Rosie was frozen.
The little, lustful men would be denied
Carnal, callisthenic excursions.
Frozen passion was never on the menu.
Not what any of them had planned
When they laced up, only this very morning
Shoe horning spit and polished brogues,
Size two platform shoes,
Très chic, très petite,
Onto their mighty, midget feet.

So Vive Rosie, Milk Wood's femme fatale,
From 33 Duck Lane. Do pop by to see her.
We really admire her sense of industry
And ability to accommodate all comers.
A legend in her own front bedroom.
We applaud her, blow her trumpet,
Sing her ribald song of praises
Louder than Organ Morgan could,
Holier than Eli Jenkins in Milk Wood Chapel,
More forcefully than PC Attila Rees might
In his police helmet, suddenly tight,
A night cap of sorts when caught short
In a most arresting dream of her.

Rosie, our rustic, busty heroine,
A woman so down to earth,
Needs honestly proclaimed
And regularly honestly satisfied
(Sometimes by quantity, if not by size)
A Salvation Army of midgets
Prays for you breathlessly,
Daily and nightly, dear Rosie P,
Under the Dingle,
Legs akimbo,
Always starry.

Stained Glass Windows Shattered

I've spent my working lifetime
Working on creating lives
Other than my own.
That's what writers do.
A funny way to pass the time,
Rhyming, scheming and plotting
Adventures for fake folk,
Who never, ever drew breath
In the real world, but simply starred
On the spotlit stage behind my eyes.

And so I know, or think I do,
A certain something
About character and motivation,
Backstory and human desire.
The limping of a damaged heart.
The rise and fall of personal histories.
It's what I do. Impure and never simple,
My very own craft and sullen art,
Practised often in dead of night,
As Dylan did, for lovers quite uninterested.

If Dylan never existed, had never
Drawn a wheezy breath in Swansea
In a year when millions were
To start their own dance of death
In mud, blood and trench-foot billets,

It would have been necessary
To invent him, to be a bantam cock,
Cocksure and strutting
In the fields of windfall light
About the house, and happy…
History gives poetic stereotypes.
Mad, bad, and dangerous
Like club-footed Lord Byron,
Or bathed in clouds of glory
Like Wordsworth, lyrically mumbling.
But later we needed someone
More modern to fit the bill
Of the twentieth-century stage.
The storyteller and versifier.
Bard and Bombast unified.

And so it was, and so it became.
Dylan Marlais Thomas came.
A middle name meaning blue,
In an old language just limping by,
And one which neither he nor I
Spoke fluently, or very much at all,
Yet both fiercely, proudly not English,
Our Welsh positivity defined
Racially by a negative, but
Keenly proud of hearth and home.
Celtic hearts, abiding.

And what was really wanted?
What did central casting
Need to deliver?
What ingenue?
What juvenile
To strut the boards in style?
All bottle green shirt,
And bombazine bombastic,
Snub-nosed, pugnacious,
A Swansea Jack Young Dog
Sniffing up Salubrious Passageway.

Vicariously we needed a no good boyo,
A schemer and hunchback dreamer,
Ready to slip his leash
And lead us on all a merry dance,
Prancing, disobedient and disorderly,
Conducting himself appallingly,
Then in a heartbeat a curly-haired cherub
Un-fallen from grace, sweet young face
Beaming in playground, park and pub,
Self-conscious Woodbine smouldering
As time ticked him onward through his years.

And he discovered, early, the wooing power of words
That called upon him, knocking on his door
In Cwmdonkin, to see if he'd come out to play,
Stalking cats and snowballing suburban conflagrations

In Wild West Sketty kitchens,
And to set adventures in short-story stone,
Sculpted, as his scrawling hands
Crawled across the paper
And fettled pages with syllables,
Written and rewritten endlessly in exercise books.

And we truly needed him to grow
And growl and lech and leach upon the world,
And in his brief encounter with life,
To act out all of Shakespeare's seven ages
In one broken-bottled night in Browns' Hotel,
Or swivelling on a White Horse barstool,
In Greenwich, NYC, playing village idiot
A little too convincingly, then dropping off his perch,
A king's canary, a miner's bird, sniffing air for us all
And finding the wordy world a very dangerous place.

In Biblical times, a scapegoat was laden down
Heavy, with all the sins of a town, and ceremonially
Driven out into the Judean wilderness
To die in dry parch-throated agony,
No bleating left in its dried-up throat,
But like a horned, cloven-footed Jesus,
Sent to save us all,
Take away our transgressions
And lay down its life, uncomplaining.
Some days we ask too much of artists.
Some days they sacrifice far too much for us.

Dylan said poems should be built with holes,
Into which unintended meanings could flash.
And when asked, by some prim interviewer
About the position of a writer in society,
Replied, 'Upright.' Standing. Cold sober
Like some sombre judge. Solemn
As a black-capped sentence-singer
Sending men down. Poetic feet of clay
Dancing, pigeon-toed, a tango upon air.
Dead men dangling, as a bad example.

Dylan did not die for my sins, or yours.
He died for his own. And he had plenty,
But balanced out with Celtic kindness,
Chaos, confusion and creativity too.
Mitigating circumstances, Your Honour,
Sitting high upon the bench. Blind justice.
Dylan rhymed in innocent expectation
That time would be kind and forgive him.
Smiling, surrounded by a pile of pebble poems,
Stained glass windows shattered around feet of clay.

Worm's Head

I was trapped on The Worm once: I had gone on it early
in the afternoon with a book and a bag of food and, going to the very,
very end, had slept in the sun…And when I woke, the sun
was going down…I ran over the rocks. The tide had come in.
I stayed on that Worm from dusk till midnight, sitting on the top grass,
frightened to go further in because of the rats and because
of the things I am ashamed to be frightened of.

Dylan Thomas

Maybe it is in the scheme of things
That a son should outstrip his father,
Though I never did. Another story.
But my son did, and here's evidence.

Judging the tides to perfection,
He walked along a dragon's broken back,
All sharp and slippery rock
Projecting out into the sea at Rhossili.

Worm's Head. I never, ever made it to the tip,
Though I feel I should have tried and trod
In Dylan's leather shod footsteps,
Scuffed brown brogues, and frayed laces.

Dylan walked and somehow even scrambled
To the very end, where Atlantic gales swirled,

Peering in sea caves where earlier poets wrote,
But where black rats now scampered. Seabirds died.

A good idea at the time. The consequences:
Stranded from dusk to midnight moon,
As the cockle-shaking slow, black sea
Outran him, took him for a Swansea fool.

And fool he was, and once below a time
Punch-drunk with words, shadow boxing,
Fighting with pugilistic phantoms and things
Of which he was sore afraid, but never named.

And we all have our unfair share
Of daylight fear and darkness, fearfully dreaming
Of riding saddled nightmares, whinnying
Over the Dingle starry, fox hunting ghosts.

I have a photographic mark of Sam's victory.
My son, a conquering hero, came
One hot August day, and triumphed
And surely touched the Pillars of Hercules.

And did they find sea caves, scraped out
Like nostrils on a sleeping dragon's head?
And did they hear, beneath Gower waves,
Drowned bells, calling like an Angelus?

No. There was no Angelus Domini. Not for Dylan,
Nor for me, though my slight indiscretions lie buried
Beneath golden sands of anonymous rhyming time,
Not anatomised, laid bare by tell-tale biographies.

But at least Dylan and my son, Sam, made it.
They both stood, tired and tempting fate and fire,
Balanced on a Welsh dragon's nose. Then strolled away,
Bathed in holy Celtic magic, for souls who walk the walk.

All long gone now. Coming up for seventy years,
Give or take a stanza or two. Dylan. A lifetime
Of rhyming and telling tall tales that seem so true,
Waiting on an imminent birthday. Slowly older.

I may never walk in the slurred footsteps of the Young Dog,
Or know the Old Dog's' tricks. Or emulate the graceful leaps
Of my own bounding blood, bottled in my son's young body.
But Sam's photograph unites us three, across sand-blown ages,

Connected by a picture from of an angle I've never seen,
But rejoice that Dylan and my son have, and told the story
Of Wales glimpsed while riding on a sleeping dragon,
Wales witnessed while walking on a blind Worm's Head.

Laugharne

Enough sunsets
Settling down,
Nestling behind
The far horizon,
Disappearing rays
Bathing the fine line
Between today going,
And tomorrow yet to come.
In between, the colour of real night-time
Fights to be born. Black light struggles
And needs to shine. Black shadows
Need boldly to steal a march
Into a world that child-like
Waits for goodnight kisses,
Dark prayers and shady alleluias,
Exclamations and exhortations
To mark and manifest an end of days,
As we gaze, wide-eyed and watching,
Our truant pupils fixed. Mitching.
Bound for our nocturnal ramblings,
Counting black sheep gambolling
Fleeced in deep sleepy black meadows,
A world where eyeless we can see,
And no shadows ever frighten us,
As on hearing Reverend Eli Jenkins'
Sunset Prayer, we make our way
Fingertip by crawling, pious fingertip,

Brave braille adventurers, touchingly
Climbing mountains of dreams,
Scheming, blind leading the blind,
Just like Captain Cat adventuring
Upon a sea of coal-black sea-horses
Whinnying, jangling bridle-black reins
Bits jingling upon a Milk Wood trip,
A journey without map or compass,
As we trot then gallop towards morning
And a new day comes dawning,
Yawning sunlight behind our backs,
Over our shrugged shoulder, in the east sky,
Sunshine singing matins as with harmony
And familiar dawn chorus ringing,
Singing from the same Genesis hymn sheet,
In the beginning was the Word.
Sunlight fresh from far away Cardiff
Steals over Carmarthenshire's holy hills,
Springing forth. And in that new day starting,
And time and rip tide, that one word rhymes
With another, and yet a flotsam other still,
Filling the tide-turning wordless world
With a birthday gift of new day's poetry.
Words are resurrected from the tomb of night,
No rolled boulder capable of ever sealing the grave
Where like some brave newborn simile saviour
Sun light Poesy rose, to serve, then save us all.

Under an Old Welsh Sky

(A Birthday Poem for Dylan Thomas)

'About time. What kept you?'
'I don't know,' I reply. 'Life, I expect.'
'Lucky you, having a life to live,'
He says, sadly, gazing over mudflats
At bored herons and an unremarkable sky.

'You're not really here,' I say. 'Long gone.'
'Indeed,' he replies. 'But here is all I know
Of a happy place, a space where
Once I fraternised with words,
Courted my muse
And nobody batted a rheumy eye
As I looked seawards, skywards
For inspiration amongst
The soft Welsh raindrops.'

'You're waxing a bit lyrical,'
I interject. 'Wordy in life,
But in death you're really expected
To hold your tongue a bit better
Apart from the contractual ghostly wailings.'

'Who can see me?'
He asks, anxious and quietly.
I break the sad news.
No one's looking anymore.

No children knocking at his door
To see if Dylan's coming out to play.
No dens to make in faraway Cwmdonkin.
No jelly, cake or bright red balloons today.

'But it's my birthday,' he exclaims.
'So what? Grow up. Birthdays are for kids
And, to be clinically accurate,
For flesh and blood people with beating hearts
Not wrecked, worm-pilfered bodies
Of once below a time boily boys like you,
Eternally sleeping off a bender
Under the unimpressed trees
Beneath a simple wooden cross
In an overgrown Welsh churchyard.'

'But think of the tourists,
Especially the Japanese.
They seek me here, they seek me there,
Take pictures of me everywhere,
Even the shadows of my shadows
And of the dust upon my
Carefully posed, untidy desk.'

'Don't they have the papers
Where you are? Do you watch the news?
To hell in a handcart, we're all bound.
The saggy bottom's fallen out
Of the tortured genius market.'

But then I feel cruel. Even the dead
Feel the pain of the selfishly still alive,
And in Dylan's puppy dog eyes
I spy a genuine despair at being forgotten.
He stands and squints and peers outside
As if waiting for a chummy Angel Gabriel,
But all he sees are dark clouds
Gathering to rain on his parade,
If only he still had one worth the droppings..

'But wait,' I say, my comforting hand
Passing through his ectoplasmic arm.
'What for?' he replies.
'For me to tell you, on this, your date of birth,
That had you not walked upon the earth,
I doubt I would have written one single poem,
Let alone all my plays, cartoons, radio dramas,
Television programmes and film scripts.'

I pause for a dramatic moment, then continue.
'Once I came to find you, years ago,
In not so swinging sixties Wales,
Knocking on your door, in my mind anyway,
Asking if Dylan could come out to play?
And you did. Poems, of which you were
A bizarre midwife, popped out of me,
Fully grown, and my fluent tongue
Won me the love of many a young woman.

A half smile flickers on his lips.
Perhaps the boy done good after all.
Oh yes. Forget all the brilliant, dense verses,
Under Milk Wood, and those childhood stories.
'You inspired me to be become a poet and a lover.
I became a writer. That was my life's highway.
And for that I owe you a debt of gratitude.'

Even though no-one has turned up
For his solitary, spectral birthday party,
I take from my pocket, and blow up,
A red balloon, and then a warm Mars Bar.
We stick in a small candle and light it,
And looking at the reflection of its tiny flame
Dancing in the truant boy's pupils
Of Dylan's squinting eyes,
I ask him to make a wish.
And then he blows out the flame.

In Laugharne darkness
Dylan disappears,
Leaving me alone,
Just another ageing poet
Talking to the blank wall
Under an old Welsh sky.

A Mumbles Odysseus

'Where's he to?'
Asked the man.
'I thought he
Was over by there,
But when I got over by here
He'd gone and buggered off.

'Of course he owes me money.
Naturally. I come here today
Expecting to be paid, at least a bit.
Twp I was, to travel here, mind,
All the way down from Mumbles
More in hope than expectation,

'But I just had to try.
Don't talk to me about kids.
I've got kids too.
Little mochyns. Little pigs.
They have mouths needing feeding
Just as much as any of his three.

'Beyond a joke, mun.
All well and good
To play the poet
But not at the price
Of other people's children
Going hungry. It's not right.

'I knew him as a kid in Sketty.
Skinned our knobbly knees together,
Climbed trees to scrump apples,
Made daring dens in Cwmdonkin,
And I ran much faster than him,
Though he won the Swansea Mile.

'Talked about me, he did. As a kid
In Christmas stories full of snowballs
And visits to sandy seashores.
Enough to make him a few bob
From the BBC Wireless, up in London,
None of which he shared with me.

'Bunked off school with him, I did,
To play marbles along the gutter,
Alleys played in blind alleyways,
And rolling along pee-stained pavements,
Happy as the glassy day was long,
As the sun rolled down into Swansea Bay.

'Got drunk with him. Well, who didn't?
Down Salubrious Passage, young whippets
In heat for beer and the occasional
Flash of a petticoat against a red brick wall.
Smiled, like him, at the unclimbable ladies,
Young mountaineers both, with short ropes.

'And in many Whitsun Treat charabancs
We would gambo and wend our way,
And later in the day come back weary
From Porthcawl, Mecca of us Mumbles mob,
A place of stolen kisses and sticky toffee apples
And being sick all along the long way home.

'There's talk in Swansea Station,
And some think it's Gospel, mind,
They're putting on special train excursions
Just for his creditors to travel and find him.
But it's the fruit of too much pop.
Laugharne hasn't even got a station.

'What's that, butty? Come close.
My ears are not so good at hearing
Things I don't want to hear.
America! God help! Not again.
He's been before. Surely he's seen it?
Making a pig of himself, make no mistake.

'America. It's a real mystery.
How can they ever understand his accent,
And ramblings about our childhood?
Secrets, they were. Boyhoods betrayed.
Still, I take my hat off. Good for him.
Nice work if you can get it, anyway.

'Expected back? No idea, you say?
I've come all this way to corner him
In his writing hut, his little den,
But again the fox has outfoxed us.
One bit of me is tamping mad,
But the scrumping kid inside smiles.

'Is that the time? Indeed it is.
No point knocking anymore
On a door destined never to be opened.
Still, perhaps I'll wander up the lane,
Knock hard on the Boat House door
And see if Caitlin's got the kettle on.

'We'll share a cup of strong Welsh tea,
And maybe tell tall tannin tales,
And drink a two-sugared toast
To our mumbling Mumbles Odysseus returning
From across the wide, wild, wicked Western Ocean,
To reclaim his waiting, long-suffering Penelope.

Bound for Far Valparaiso

In the Beginning and the Ending
Was the never-ceasing Word,
Beginning when the first light blinked,
Ending when all the lights failed and faded,
Though omnipresent neon bright-washed
Your hospital pallid paleness, as you lay
Unaccompanied and waiting for the hand
To take you by it, and lead you to the land
Of the Garden that had never left you,
Though you believed that you had long left it,
Behind its iron railings, all neatly packed away
Like unwanted gifts after Christmas Day,
All boxed away, safe, sound and secret.

It was a future that, until today, you thought
You'd never see, or need to use,
Until, in NYC, you squarely ran out of time,
Ran out of rope and hope and found your feet
Dancing on air like a highwayman,
Turned off by the unforgiving gibbet,
Dangling, dying, for all the rubber-necking world
To see and gawp, ward wide open to public glare,
Until the shroud man come to wash you clean
For the final voyage you would soon be making.

No farewells, no infamous last words,
For now your ersatz extended family,

The sad menagerie of dramatic characters
That all we writers raise, suckle and hand-feed
From embryos to sad-sack cadavers,
All come, invisible, to say goodbye,
Standing, unseen, at your gurney bedside,
While stiff and starched nurses bustle
And in the scalding white light of death
Kindly close your bulging eyelids,
Switch off your star in the firmament.
As now the ball you threw into the Cwmdonkin sky,
All those years ago, silently starts to fall back to earth,
To find a final resting place amongst the shrubbery,
Glades, and the captive trees of your old playground,
A place where the light of childhood never fades.

Despite the going down of Swansea sun
In all the dusky dens and secret spots,
Even after the turning of keeper's key,
We will always fond and foolishly think
We hear your voice echoing in darkness.
A strawberry boy, joy quite uncontainable,
Who even as the final spotlight went out
Still found a childhood place to cwtch,
A hutch, your precious hunchback kennel,
Till the morning of Salvation's dawning,
When all the earth will open wide to welcome
Dylan to rest and dream forever, and try to make
New fibs and silly stories to amuse blind worms
Who, with tender braille, see eye to eye with him.

And, cheekily he winked at Mr Death, the Parkie,
And secretly planned one final great adventure.
Just like a Swansea Peter Pan, Dylan Thomas ran,
Second star to the right, straight on till morning,
Sailing all the tickled-trout-filled rivers of windfall light.
Then at night, exhausted, with no extra time to play,
Came home, back to number No. 5 Cwmdonkin Drive,
To sleep eternity away, up in his single bed of dreams,
Serenaded by soft sea-sounds sung by Swansea Bay.
A sea choir singing for him, as with Blind Captain Cat,
They cast off, and together set sail. Bound for far Valparaiso,
For adventures not yet born, and poems not yet written.

Sargasso Sea

'Prepare to meet thy God'
Framed upon the Boathouse mantle,
Embroidered by nimble fingers,
A sentiment of other times.
But was attention ever paid
To this Puritanical exhortation
In a house so often riven
By love's loving complications?
Two free spirits, finding that freedom
Is anything but free.

No one teaches the art of love,
Though vainly we might try to map
And measure out our damp dreams.
We all set out as virgin souls,
Innocents, however fumbling
Our tumbling self-defence might be.
We try our level best at faithfulness,
Hoping that if we are doomed to fail,
Out of sight, a blind eye will be turned.

'Is that bloody man dead yet?' Caitlin's words.
One report of her bittersweet bitterness
Upon your final New York arrival.
Close enough to make no difference,
But not close enough to feel distance.
Atlantic miles and so many seductive smiles.

Too many convenient, intimate strangers.
Two lifetimes spent in consensual blindness
Like dear Captain Cat. Happier to sail
Love's old oceans and the Sargasso Seas,
Caught up in seaweed-strewn memories,
Long since ensnared. Trapped, becalmed,
As all hands, they puffed and blew their empty sails,
Trying, and spectacularly failing, ever to break free.

A Tale of Two Blind Captains

All night pale rain has fallen,
Surfing the invisible west wind.
Outside my rattling windowpanes
New leaves dance to age-old tunes
Carried on the musical breeze,
And Wales, place of my birth,
Land of my Fathers, lurks unseen
Behind a thick, dawn greyness.
The River Severn remains shrouded,
The bridges only slowly appearing
Like weary teenagers, reticent to rise.

Set in for the day, common sense says.
Computer wizardry confirms the hunch.
'Percentage of predicted precipitation'
Rains across my iPad tablet screen,
As BBC forecasts parade before my eyes.
Not really needed. I've seen rain before.
Seventy years of being a damp target.
It doesn't get any better over a long life,
Though once below a time, as Dylan said,
Young children might leap from 1950s beds,
Dreaming and scheming of puddle jumping,
Splashing, feet galoshed in Woolworth wellies.

This is a day of unpredictable weather,
As I lie in my storm-tossed bed

Thinking about uplifting tea to come.
I remark about it in this damp poem
As blind Captain Cat below the Dingle,
Starry with ominous comets, quite unseen,
Calls out foul weather warnings to his ghostly crew.
But old sea-dog him, he'd really make very little
Of tiny typhoons that stalk my River Severn,
Back upstream of squally Milk Wood.
In his early thirties, young straying Cat sailed
The Roaring Forties. My tiny rain simply doesn't matter.

No need to put on a yellow sou'wester,
Or slip on skidding oil skins, to slide across the deck
Of dear old SS *Kidwelly*, bound for far Bilbao,
Belly bursting with cargo, stashed tight, safe and sound,
Dreaming of Rosie Probert and tight holds.
This weak tea, rainy day will not capsize me,
Or worse run me bare-arsed ragged, off Cape Finistère.
My Bay of Biscuits beckons, and as I dunk my digestive,
With my still sleepy, sand-dust eyes, I spy blind cataracts
And whirlpools swirling in my early morning tea.
My own day will be lived, charted, on dry land.
Sea salt peril will not stalk upon my Gloucestershire hillside.
Meanwhile, in Laugharne, non-conformist rain
Apologises, politely, with every drop that tumbles.
West of Mumbles, even the weather goes to chapel
And knows its place, face clean, as every holy droplet

[85]

Remembers it was once a bit part player in the Flood
That bore Noah up, and sent him sailing, searching
For safe harbour, finally grounding on Mount Ararat.
As a child, I was always puzzled
Since a chapel with that very name, Ararat,
Sat on the flat on my beloved Whitchurch Common.
Where had the mount bit gone? I often wondered,
As I played jumpers for goalposts with my chums.

I played with all my shipmate teammates,
Corporeal, and real as any long-drowned
Ghostly strawberry boys who once sailed ships
In the gravel-filled Cwmdonkin fountain,
Dylan's magical playground, the park,
Dear to him as Whitchurch Common to me.
Treasure hunt any pirate poet's past,
Look for the X that marks the spot,
Where beneath shifting sands of time
A battered trunk of memories, dreams
And bejewelled early words are to be found,
And you'll find it, castaway,
Marooned in a solitary childhood.

Tea drunk, biscuits keel-hauled,
And now sailing the peristaltic waves
Of my alimentary canal, I resolve to set out
Into my own day. The rain has stopped,
And even now the wind-blown leaves

Perform a slower dance, as if smooching.
I rise, and peering west, my eyes grow bright
At the sight of Wales fast being revealed,
Early mists burning off and disappearing,
And way down the lucky Severn, far westward ho,
In Milk Wood, sleepy people come and go,
Oblivious to the fact they don't really exist.

Swan Song

As if by serendipity
The image and title arrives.
Florence, a virtual friend,
(Coincidentally the name
Of Dylan's mother)
Writes, expressing concern
I might be burning my poetic candle
At both ends. And she's right.
I might be. So I resolve
To take a break from Poesy,
But first turn my attention to just this one,
One of my growing, rambling sequence,
Poems inspired by the life, lies and fictions
Of Dylan Thomas.

And it has been a long voyage
These last months before the mast,
Casting around for tales that tell
The point and purpose of my exploration
And explanation why I first set sail
And how now I plan to dock again
Finding my home port with gratitude.
I need my final poems to be
Neat lines across my Captain's Log,
Inscribed so firmly even blind Cat
Could see and realise we had landed
Safe and sound in Swansea town.

In my ancient mariner's mind,
No albatross slain, no call to stoppeth
By innocent passers-by, one in three,
With eyes, sea salt and vinegary
Up Salubrious Passage, after dark.

But I feel this is the time and place, Dylan,
To speak of your mother.
Here's me, always historically
A daddy's boy, just like you.
After all, he was the one for whom
You wrote your 'Do Not Go Gentle'.
If memory serves, no verse exists
For the one who supplied coffee
And sandwiches, daily to fuel
Your late-night writing excursions,
Who regularly subbed you a quid or two,
And who, until you were twenty-one,
Ran a knife along your boiled egg top
For her pride and joy. Her little boy.
Her daughter's young brother.
Who once put her Welsh Mam foot in it
With your new girlfriend, sophisticated Pam,
When she let slip your real age.
A very young dog indeed. A puppy on heat.

And now, as I steer and stare out for Mumbles
And safe home, as the sailor's cry sounds,

I think of another nautical expression,
A toast known to generations of old tars
Onboard ships, or in sailors' bars worldwide:
'To wives and lovers. May they never meet!'
And you did very wily well at keeping secrets.
Writers can conjure up many mysteries
And pull so many rabbits out of top hats,
And what is there left to say about you
As I clear my poetic throat
To sing your Swansea Swan Song?
Mythologically and biologically incorrect,
Since swans are not mute, and monogamous,
And don't wait to save the best till last.

No, we have a far quieter farewell to say,
Like two old friends interrupted by a tumour,
As happened to me with my dear chum Chris.
We all reach a point beyond which we
Walk Indian file, no longer side by side,
But if I look behind I can still see you,
Though death makes you dawdle, just a bit.
The time has almost come
To stop my ghostly conversations.

My last toast singing in your ear,
Our Swan Songs sung, our bridges burnt,
I call the crew up on the deck
And check the tar-caulked shroud

That soon will cwtch and cuddle you,
Full fathom five, deep within the ocean,
Where coral is waiting for you.
And I will then sail on alone
For as long as my forever might be,
To try to find new poetic songs to sing
In whatever time is left to me for rhyming.

Captain Cat Sets Sail Again

Sea-monster?
Viking longship?
Neither. The *Helvetica*,
Nineteenth-century wreck.
Sand locked,
Barnacle pocked,
Sailing yesterday's seas,
Crewed by ghosts
Running up the rigging.
Rounding Worm's Head
Or trying to make it.
Scraping a crusty sand scalp
And tumbling, all hands
On deck, spirits diving deep
But saved from Davy Jones,
Rescued from their bones
Being ground down to powder.

A hundred years and more
Sitting here. Snapped and captured
In countless photograph albums,
Backdrop to many Rhossili Sundays,
Kids rock-pooling in her stern,
Playing pirates in her broken bow,
Jolly Rogering to hearts' content,
Dylan's wild and strawberry boys,
Guilty in their holy innocence,

Young hunchback-dogs, happily playing,
Baying at an Ancient Mariner's moon.
Press ganged. Shanghaied. Taken by tides.
This is a place of sea-swept yesterdays.
One moonlight night, Blind Captain Cat
Will tap his way up from Llareggub
And come aboard, in uniform finery,
Piped on to the phantom foredeck,
And set sail, with his old ghostly crew.
Hoist the invisible mainsail.
Haul anchor. Simply disappear.

And leave nothing here,
But soft golden Gower sand,
Boat bones picked clean
And plucked by time's teeth,
Leaving behind a blind worm
And the night sky high above.

On my Way to Hollywood

'Dearest Cat,
This time it's working,
Or will, when I can get there,
To the land of oranges and sun.
Then everyone will get paid
With lots left over, dear love,
And dearest lover.
Toys for both the boys,
A dolly for Aeronwy,
And maybe a new frock for you,
And our hearty cockles warmed.
Cold beer in Browns
And money. Lots left over.
Cwtched safe, under the mattress.
And nights of loving, like it used to be,
Before I became big and bloated
And a waste of space around the place.
This time it will all come to pass.
I know. This time it's working.

This time it's working. I've just seen him.
Stravinsky. Igor, I must learn to call him.
In his NYC hotel room. The Copley Plaza.
He wasn't well. Had a cold, or something.
Room service brought us drinks.
Him, squeezed orange juice from California,
Golden as the sun that is young once only,

And me a Scotch. Never too early in the day.
We played together, nicely, as they say.
Auden had put in a good word, or three,
And honestly I think the old man liked me.
What? I hear you questioning. An opera.
There's posh. There's intellectual.
And we can. And me. I'll do it. Honestly,
In two shakes of a Mumbles moggy's tail.
Got the story. Subject. Neat and tidy.
And it can be spawned in weeks, not months.
A brand new dawn, birthed in California.
My West Coast resurrection. My sunny rebirthing.
This time it's working.

'End of the world in an atomic accident…'
Environmental Emergency. You see,
I know it doesn't sound a barrel of laughs,
But listen, hear what we mean to make of it.
Apocalyptic, but promising hope for new happenings.
A new Adam and new Eve. A Nevada desert Eden
Where dusty rocks, plants and atomic-tested trees
Will all sing in harmony. All these new beginnings
Exalt, exulting in appreciation of a second chance.
And there might be dancing too. Why not?
And the plot? The libretto would all be mine.
Bigger and better than *Milk Wood*, anyway.
Something to stand the test of ticking time.

Something proper. Not just a play for voices
But real opera, with my words neatly scored.
A try and a conversion worthy of the Arms Park.
No, I know, Cat, that I'm not naturally musical.
But what can be so hard? As Reverend Eli cried,
'Praise God we are a musical nation.' Me too.
So it's settled. After New York I will go and stay
In Los Angeles, with Igor. Eager to make magic.

Boston University. They're paying for it all.
Auden and Igor did Rake's Progress for them.
Opened the door, so I can squeeze in. Tidy.
No. That was a joke. Rotund as ever. Sadly.
But I'll soon fly away to the City of Angels
And ring the cracked Angelus Bell, to toll the knell
Of poverty passing, for ever and ever. Amen.
He's even built an extra room on to his house, Igor.
I'll stay there while we're collaborating.

And I will drink in sunshine and fresh oranges.
I'll get healthy and regain my athletic best,
Fit as a butcher's pup, or old School Mile champion.
So that's about it. Caitlin, I'll love and leave you,
As I always do. But in the future won't, so much.
Next time you hear from your peripatetic rhymer
There'll be sunny stamps upon an air mail envelope,
And you can simply imagine me sipping iced Russian tea
Upon some far flung veranda. Or porch, I think they call them.

This time it's working. Have no doubt of that, my Cat.
New words soon will be flowing from my old sunburnt brain.'

Poem to a Clay Man

Almost time to go.
Time to draw a line
Across the page.
Shut up the exercise book
And look for something else.
Let you mulch and moulder
In your overgrown leafy grave,
Or limp between the pages
Of your spine-damaged books.

You never planned on immortality.
In fact you worked hard to avoid it.
When not otherwise engaged
You filled spindrift pages
With pencil arachnids,
Spidery words crawling
From deep mind depths,
Through the soul's plughole
With bombastic, hirsute glee.

A working stiff. Sometimes a hack
Racking up lines. Prose by the inch,
Penny Dreadful stories
Mined from childhood memories.
Like so many you wrote
To try to put pennies over your eyes.
You also rhymed to praise God.
Songs of Lack of Innocence
Psalms of Bad Experiences.

No Sketty William Blake, but given to visions
Hiding in the rye recesses of a tormented soul,
Like Swansea town, you were both ugly and beautiful
In frustrating parts, with a heart as large as forever is,
And deep darkness, deep down, where bareback,
You rode your nightmares. Galloped once too often
And overplayed your hand, that signed your own papers.
What does it matter which particular shot got you?
You were killed by death. No other doctor's note needed.

I have rhymed you so many times.
Knocked your door to see if you were coming out to play.
But no more. In a modern world beyond feverish imaginings,
Words have lost their killing power and seem like blanks.
Triggered by desire and loneliness, craving simply to touch,
We fire our stanza salvos into the air, like rebels, celebrating.

Do you care? Or are you too far gone? Meat for slow worms
That, even now, squirm where your heart once beat.
Or has acid soil and rich Welsh clay modelled you anew,
Sculpted as well as any hunchback's hand could do?
One night, over bosky Sir John Hill as the moon rises,
Will you rise again too? Some long-delayed clay
Jesus resurrected, to complete one last lyric,
Then crumble back to earth, letting snowdrops drip
And daffodils delight in bright floral Laugharne sunlight?

Where will I be on that day of all too brief rebirth
And then your endless dissolution? Who can say?

I don't know, my dear, dead, imaginary friend.
Perhaps, having made my bed as well,
I'll be lying in it finally. Fibbing and telling
Tall stories of my own, to sepulchral bookworms
Gliding and squirming over my once bright pupils.
Or maybe gourmet maggots seeking haute cuisine
Will be making a meal of me, and burping, softly.
We'll see, won't we. On the final day I join you
For our last supper ...

Blowing Out The Lights

(In Memory of Aeronwy)

'Just one more,' he called out to me,
But of course, I knew he was lying.
Perhaps he was trying to break the record
For most brain-deadening whiskies
Drunk in a single sitting, though mostly
He was slouched, or barely propped up.

I watched the lights behind his eyes turn off,
Like Milk Wood readying for sleep,
But sadly there was no Reverend Jenkins
Here in New York's White Horse tavern,
To pour out shots of Christ's healing blood.
Just a bored barkeeper not even keeping score.

'Come on. Let's go and play in the park.'
'But it's dark,' said Dylan.
'Central Park's full of muggers and buggers and…'
'Poets?' I said. 'No, let's go to Cwmdonkin,
Back home. Safe and sound in Swansea town.'

And for one singing moment,
A single light flickered on again
At the mere mention of the magic name,
The place where as a boy he came
To dream away the hours in play
And throw balls of hope, up into the high sky.

But then seeing the whisky glass empty,
The barman fired another round,
And Dylan, like a condemned man,
Blind drunk, blindfolded, faced the firing squad.
When the swigged shot hit, I saw him slump,
Then sag a little lower. On his way.

Return Journey 2022

Today, I will rise and go again,
By bus and early morning train,
To where, once, I called home,
And which was, and in a way,
Will always be, and through time
Proved well worthy of the name.

Seventy plus years have passed,
And I ask myself the question,
'If you take the boy out of Wales,
Does something of Wales stay behind?'
Like a benign and loving splinter
You're happy to have beneath your skin?

Each morning when dawning birds
Sing me awake in an unseen choir,
I draw back bedroom curtains,
And west across the dark Severn River,
See Wales silhouetted on my skyline,
In my waking eye-line. Happily in the way.

Today my train will speed uncomplaining
Under Severn's waters, and I will surface
In another country. No need to hold my breath.
I will rattle over awoken sleepers
Along miles of track, back to Cardiff,
A lovely, beloved city. Once my hometown.

Arriving at once tipsy Central Station,
Which once below a time stank happily of brewery,
My brain slips back to childhood memories.
Growing up in Talygarn Street, playing on pavements
Before time ticked and tore me away, one 1950s day,
To play on Whitchurch Common, young and innocent.

Today I am doing a very grown up thing:
Visiting a publisher, carrying years of dreams
Inside a bag upon my sometimes sagging shoulder.
Poems written for Dylan T, hopefully destined to see
The light of day, as I once did, in September sunshine,
Poetic children sent toddling, to play long after I am gone.
Cardiff town, you gave me my first lungful of life.
A childhood loved and loving, full of family and friends,
And my awakening to the possibilities of learning,
The ache of yearning for girls, for whom my young pen
Poured out praises, as I gazed, with childlike appreciation
That never ages, across my early poetic pages.

Tonight I will finish the day exactly where now I start,
In my West Country bed, weary and looking back
At where the sun sets over Severn waters. Into Wales.
And I will know again, what 'hiraeth' means,
As into dreams, I smuggle new contraband memories,
Old pictures that I will see again, when I go home.

Sunset Prayer

Eight o'clock on an English, autumn Monday,
Already I have bathed and taken to my bed.
Outside, overhead, dark skies arrived unheard
An hour ago, bringing cheeky raindrops
Bouncing off my clay-tiled, tired old roof,
Plopping deep in deep dark puddles,
Falling between cracks of leaking guttering
That, faithfully, I promised to get mended.

Growing old in a house far older than me,
Sash windows rattle, fit less well than once.
Wooden frames let in rainwater,
And carpets reflect the passage of old feet
And tiny, tripping toes, as my child grew
And trod, and dropped, his glorious way
To adulthood, then fatherhood himself.
Now my granddaughters tread in his footprints.

A sensible Edwardian space. High ceilings,
Steep staircase. Sensible brick garden wall.
And just like the house, sometimes I recall
That I feel the want of a lick and promise of paint,
A tile or two replacing. Three score and ten
Has come, and gone, but I'm still sheltering here
And seeing long days ending, in descending suns.

Once upon a time I was called a des-res.
My cheeks flushed with a sense of adventure.
My shining windows were soulful blue.
But time mists. Condensation happens.
Cobwebs grow unseen in all four corners,
And round about midnight, slugs quarrel
Over a cat bowl on the kitchen floor.

My house and me, we may no longer be ideal,
Yet we are all we've got. We deserve each other,
Through rain and sun and hail and snow,
Perched high up on a hillside, village down below,
Overlooking fields, Severn River and Wales,
Land of My Fathers, but also Land of me,
Though for five decades I've been masquerading,
Uncomplaining, as a Gloucestershire Man.

Not Milk Wood maybe, but nice here.
A good enough place to grow and sink
Into the western sky, and one day to die.
And every evening the sun does just that.
As like the Reverend Eli Jenkins
I say an endless Sunset Prayer
As I watch sun set, and drop into its grave,
Cwtched well in behind my old Welsh hills,
To be resurrected, each new day dawning.
When my ticked off time finally comes,
I will unceremoniously rise to meet the skies,

Like countless winters, when roaring wood fires
Cremated oak and apple, coloured the air,
Painting my name up, from my pen-nib chimney
And blew me, nightly, across Welsh skies.

Nine o'clock on an English autumn Monday,
And I am reclining in my king-sized bed,
Aching. Heels cracked with too much mileage,
A small bottle of soporific lavender
Ready to be sprinkled on my pillow
To ease the way to sleep. Eventually,
When I have set the world to rights
By writing my poetic farewell to the day,

Not Under Milk Wood's final prayer,
Filled to the brim with agnostic Hallelujahs,
But mine. Unsure and uncertain of a resurrection,
But with the new day already creeping on its way,
As its embryonic rays of coming sunshine loiter
And meander on the face of the spinning sphere,
Hopefully to reach me, here, in hours to come,
And find my house, still standing, for another day.
For this, and that, at least, I give thanks and pray
As this day dies down to country sleep.

Daydreaming, with Seagulls, over Swansea Bay

Desktop. Beer bottle bookend.
Milk Chocolate fading
And battered spines
Of poetry books, leaning,
Learnt helpless, on a desk.
Is this reconstruction real?
A feeling that it might be
But who knows? Poetic clothes
Long disappeared or discarded.
A Cardigan, knitted clothing
(Not a West Wales place)
And if walls could talk
This room would squawk
A beakful. A parrot cage.
A rage against the dying.
A trying, mostly succeeding place.
A space upstairs. A single bed
And straight back chairs,
'Comfy', not really necessary.
(New born words don't need
To sit around, staring.)
Cut their umbilicus.
Check their infant lungs
Have power to pray, and curse, in verse.
Syllables keeping syllables company.
Metaphors toddling and tottering.
Not yet drunk. Play acting inebriation to come

When words will be travelling companions home,
Climbing uphill from the pub,
Looking for a tidy Welsh front garden
Where, fit to burst, Brains rain will fall
And tell tall stories to hardy perennials,
Plants who knew such stories well.
When once asked about the 'position'
Of the writer in society, Dylan replied,
'Upright,' in a well rehearsed contradiction,
Fiction, since poor dab, he often wasn't able
To walk the walk, or totter the talk,
After preening, like a Sketty Peacock,
For a night down town, downing pints
Smoking self-conscious Woodbines
Wreathed in a man-made miasma
Of his making. Incense shrouding
As he walked in his beer stained chasuble
Making up secular hymns and anthems
Bound to stand the test of rhyming time
For as long as forever might be.
Taking tea with Rupert Brooke
Sailing with Yeats to Byzantium
Across Swansea Bay, for good,
To find far horizons, and eventually
Reach the world's lip, there to trip
And slip and slide, to plunge to places
From which there was no return,

Leaving behind spindrift pages
And floating fragments.
Scatterings upon the cold waters
For seagulls to wheal and take and catch,
Snatches of poetic sounds spread out
Upon a Sargasso Sea, weed clogged with words.
Mysterious, these discarded,
Hard-earned images and mental pictures,
Just flotsam and jetsam, once the tide turned,
And there was no First Voice or Narrator,
Just seagulls, their beaks full of the griefs
Of ages, and sea-salt pages, as they bobbed
Upon the fishing boat crowded waters,
Close to where curlews pray and gannets gobble,
Where once below a time
You imagined and created stories,
Every day, in a beer bottle bookend bedroom
Daydreaming, with Seagulls, over Swansea Bay.

Dreaming of Eden

Since time's first tick,
Though back in time
Time was not mechanical
But moved more quietly,
Across deaf heavens,
The planets wandering
And the shifting sun shone,
Time, and the seasons
And all of mankind danced
To the music of the spheres,
And rolling years seemed eternity.

But what was always constant,
And a striving desire to attain
By common man, and common artist,
Was the road back to a place
Where once we knew, in our hearts
If not our empty, echoing heads.
The way back to the Garden. Our Eden.
Different, but the same somehow,
To every soul who traced their ancestry
Back to that place of Adam, Eve and Snake.

Awakening. Genesis trumpeting
And 'In the Beginning, was the Word'.
So that story started of our arrival
Then departure from paradise on earth,

Cast out, as punishment for woman's sin
And her desire, not for sensual skin and lust
But just because she disobeyed paternalistic
God the Father, and knew her own mind,
Desiring to feast upon the tree which foretold
Knowledge of Good and Evil. Enlightenment.

Due process was denied her. No court.
No jury of her peers, since she had none,
Yahweh, or so he later came to be called,
Was prosecution, jury and hanging judge.
Immovable, He who would not budge,
But just pointed to Eden's touchline,
The walk of shame and an early bath.
No right of appeal. No video referee.
Cast out for all eternity into darkness.
Zero tolerance. A compassion by-pass.

Ever since that little local unpleasantness,
The Fall, Adam's sons and Eve's daughters
Have tried to get back to the Garden
As Joni Mitchell crooned. The wound ran deep.
The shift. The schism. The Woodstock crevasse.
The schizophrenic separation. The primal pain
Only to be healed again, not by psychotropic pills
But by wishing and willing our way back home,
To find the Garden once again, though overgrown,
Hastily abandoned. Like Chernobyl, only quieter.

Throughout time, men have, indeed, sought
To walk-back history, and find harmonious rhyme,
To solve the mystery and riddle of just why
We spin, grave and gracelessly, in cold space,
Devoid of real parental and loving intercession
Preventing us jamming forks into electric plugs,
Free to bugger up the world at our wilful whim
While He, the Park Keeper, cold shoulders us
Not even throwing back our football.
Maybe God's too proud to pardon us at all.

So, artists and philosophers have dreamt schemes,
And puffed pipe dreams, to find another Eden.
A place similar in many ways, just devoid of Madam Eve
And her complicit, passive aggressive partner, Adam.
And the Serpent, naturally. And ideally free of God.
In waves of generations we've tried to locate a space
Beyond the Pillars of Hercules', a place of deep content
Where they, and we, and friends, and wives and lovers
Can sit and partake of dejeuner sur l'herbe,
Dress code formal. Or naturalistically naked.

John Milton found Paradise Lost, travelled there,
And hob-nobbed with Lucifer, an occasional visitor
From the Fallen Angels of the Underworld.
Some say Milton gave Satan all the best lines
But old John was blind, so maybe he didn't see.
Other places. Paradise Gardens, beyond dreams.

Debussy composed a piece of music called just that,
While D.H. Lawrence and his older fancy woman, Frieda,
Spent life looking for, and dreaming of a new Eden,
Though after his passing, she left his ashes on a train.

Painter Paul Gauguin felt the South Seas was the answer,
Escaping Paris, leaving behind an estranged cool wife
In Copenhagen, he sailed in search of block colours,
Primitive scenes, and disturbingly, several thirteen year olds.
Artistic license endorsed. We don't approve of his freedom.
Thomas Moore, philosopher, named it, and wrote of Utopia,
While others built fairy castles in the cloud cuckoo lands,
And Thomas Hobbes fly-fished for his Leviathan
While Swift traveled with Gulliver to a place of tiny men
And Tennyson dined with Lotos Eaters, picking food with his pen.

Samuel Butler created back to front Erewhon
(Read it in reverse, just like Dylan's Llareggub)
Whilst poet W.B. Yeats sailed off to his Byzantium
And in Lost Horizons', Hilton found ageless Shangri-La,
Far away from Orwell's 1984, where clocks struck thirteen.
Aldous Huxley finally found his Brave New World,
While Karl Marx divided up this planet of men
With his pen drawing a line between East and West,
A discredited credo, enslaving the very working millions
It was intended to liberate, from bonds and ancient shackles.

But still we try. We all long to feast upon pie in the sky
That satisfies life's hunger and creative night starvation,
And I am guilty of that too. Seeing greener pastures new,
And like many questers and nomads, sometime gettomg it wrong.
As Dylan did, a man I feel I know, though I probably don't.
Forty poems looking at his life and wanderings,
A Welsh Odysseus grumbling about his lovely, ugly town,
Seeking answers far too large for small Welsh hands to handle,
In hot beds of other men's wives, then stealing their cuckold's shirts.
Always seeking to find the Zion of the holy water bead,
Not realising that the faucet had run dry.

Finding Where My Heart Was Hiding

It was the infidelity.
The straw that broke
The camel's back.
Dylan jumping on anything
Female with a pulse,
And terrible at hiding it.

Love letters in his pocket,
I read them all of course. Tragic.
And the telephone calls,
Downstairs when I was in bed.
I said what I thought about it,
But part of him wanted to get caught.

Silly bitches sending him flowers
He passed on to me. Waste not.
The drinking I could manage. Held my end up.
Didn't always get the kid's meals on the table,
But we scraped by. I did most things,
And him. Well, he did bugger all.

Can't sugar coat it. Left me in Laugharne
Lonely weeks on end. In London
Getting his end away. Before America.
Earning from the BBC and spending it
On beer and tarts. No wonder I felt a need
To feel something inside me, occasionally.

Local oafs, but something to cling to
On Saturday nights, pints downed in Browns,
Then a forgettable nightcap under the stars.
I had to run fast just to keep up.
He kept them on the go, though God knows
What they all saw in him.

The Americans were worst.
Riding him like a bike with a flat tyre,
Then boasting to their buddies,
With impossible small bums and varsity tits
And bobbed hair. They were bloody everywhere,
While I was here, giving the kids baked beans for tea.

I raised them almost single handed. All three.
Not a paternal bone in his funny-looking body.
The problems were the stayers. I can name three,
But won't. Those who thought they were special,
Those who believed they had a place
In his heart. Give me strength!

In Italy we have a saying. Dylan was 'soft bread'.
Me, I needed someone tough. But no. Nowhere near.
But when time came for him to be taken away forever,
I knew the truth, that he was the only one who ever came
Close to finding where my heart was hiding.

Gently

And maybe some nights
We might turn the lights lower
And sit in simple silent time
And remember. Just remember.
I recall your old bones upright,
Corduroy trousers flapping in the wind
On icy winter days in the playground,
The sea of souls parting as you sailed.
And I remember songs sung at Christmas,
Carols and Music Hall refrains,
Though at times it must have pained you to hear
The ribald words behind the rhymes.
And books piled upon books, underpinning.
Books galore, some which
I read by torchlight, under winter-cold bed covers,
My trapped breath warming my shivering.
And do you ever think of days at the seaside
Before illness stole you from us, more and more?
Of charabanc trips, and even chips in paper,
Ink words adorning them? And can you recall
The day I won the Swansea Mile?
You smiled an appropriate headmaster's smile,
But later, when we stepped in through the door,
You hugged me, where no one saw.
Father, I ask these questions, and others yet to come
As I sit beside you, as you snore politely
By the fire that flickers. And can you still see fantasies

Within the glowing embers? And can you understand
The rhymes I'm spinning
Upstairs, in my solitary single bedroom
Voyaging on salty seas to Valparaiso,
Poetic feet never getting wet, sea legs dancing?
And whenever you do set
Sail, as despite my pleading I'm sure you will,
When you catch your tide, and taken at the flood,
Ride it to find your sunset, then,
When there's just emptiness occupying
The shrinking space you still take up,
Within the diminished space we all call home,
Will I drink a toast? Will I let you go?
Who knows? Who knows or can guess?
My father. My sometimes absent-minded pilot,
Will I need to learn seamanship myself,
And sail, westward, single-handed
Beyond the Pillars of Hercules?
And captain. My captain. Will I get lost?

The 39 Steps

Today I write to you, far-away Kevin,
As I do sometimes, unseen buddy
Out on the coast of sunny California,
Where Dylan, optimistically, was bound
When Mr Death tripped him up in NYC
And the Hollywood dream was ruled not to be.

Though Kevin and me have never met,
We poets tend to think and spend
Our dwindling rhyming time
Much the same: making up our tall tales,
Whether in a high house overlooking Wales,
Or in the Golden State, muses in Chevrolets.

Kevin writes back to tell me
Of his own 'Deaths and Entrances',
As long-gone Dylan called them.
A first grandchild soon to be celebrated,
A stepdad leaving the party early.
It happens to us all, everywhere, the world.

Pinging elevators in an old Woolworths store,
The sound of coming silence, more and more
As we pass, floor to floor.
We poets make a habit of spotting patterns,
As we quietly ascend to meet our makers
Or, ungently, hit the button marked 'Emergency'.

I have granddaughters. One my dear dad knew,
The other made her entrance on life's stage
A while after dad made his exit and curtain call,
And there are precious nights when I babysit
And she sees on TV the great-grandad she never met
Joking to camera, as if just to her, across the ages,

And so it is. And so it has become.
A heaven ticked around the stars.
Poets living, and poets long dead,
In feather beds, or laid in beds of clay,
And so it will be. We each try to do our bit
To honour words. Sometimes we manage.

But one thing unites us all,
Or so mindful Buddhists say:
'All sentient beings suffer'.
Colour-blind pain is the denominator.
As we soar like Dylan's ball tossed
Childhood high. Then fall back.

Just get on with it. This life of contradiction.
This mysterious 39 Steps.
Like Mr Memory in Alfred Hitchcock's film.
We try to answer random questions
Shouted out from the stalls,
And hope we manage to get some right,

Until falling darkness calls, and we must leave
The rows of silent seats behind,
Hopefully with some applause fading
In our ears, as we remove our mask
Of stage make-up and wander into the night,
Not knowing where we are bound. Our last act.

Singing My Songlines

Songlines: the trails of music and words left by ancestors
Of the Aborigines. When the ancestors rose from their sleep
During the dreamtime, they sang men into existence.
Each left a musical trail as a means of communication between men .

I sing my Songlines,
Dream my Dreaming,
Realising late in life
Poetry's true meaning,
To me and maybe others too.

I am no indigenous one.
No First Nation,
No Aboriginal Man,
Yet in ways these last dark days
Have sung me. And now I am.

In the beginning was the dreaming.
Wordless first, then accompanied
By song snatches, then more, song-lines
Tying the land together with song highways
And tuneful skyways. Mapping space and place.

If we know our true song and sing along,
And share the way with myths and tales
Of timeless times before ticking started,
We will never be lost, but through the word
Know our place. Our location to the very syllable.

Creation stories. Gods and billabongs.
Creatures that call, slither and crawl.
Birds that fly or run across the ground.

Creatures carrying bounced babies in pouches.
Or bears who are not bears at all, eating eucalyptus.

But what is any of this to occidental, accidental me?
Born in a Cardiff nursing home now a mosque,
Brought up in the 1950s, my only Outback
Whitchurch Common, fit for a hundred games
But devoid of dingo dogs, or creeping crocodiles.

The poems I began to write and then started
To write me, in rhyming time from teens
To this very moment, many thousands now,
Happily with no sign of ceasing, two thousand
Since Spring 2020, they are my dreaming.

No passport to riches or fame,
Poetry is an outback incantation
A solicitation. A sweat lodge. Spiritual soliloquies.
Hymns ancient, modern and secular.
Deals done with distant gods, to find direction.

First, a spring trickle bursting,
Designed to feed the ears and lips
Of young loves whose books I carried home,

Then grown lovers in Cambridge college rooms,
Revealing rhyming, rhythmic talents, unashamedly.

And so in the beginning, my beginning began
Spinning words hypnotised and hypnotising
By mesmerising light that flashed and flickered.
My very own spirit animal. The Word. My totem.
The sinuous curve of snake-like letter S arose.

Sleepwalking, daytime dreaming started,
Across a stretch now many decades wide,
Following invisible lines and singing songs,
Rhymes guiding. No woomera needed
To launch my spearing words. No boomerang.

I went Walkabout with poetry and still
I am out there in the Outback of my mind,
Red dust caking my eyes, still surprised at finding
So many song-lines stretching, twisting, as I stray
From my own inner Uluru, to my poetic Byron Bay.

And on the way I've made friends
With wriggling words. When hungry,
Grammatical grubs have filled me up,
And I've feasted on the manna of metaphor.
Cracked poem bones open. Ate their marrow
And drunk my fill from word rivers, sated.

I've replicated real life with graphic squiggles,
Caught letters like so many scurrying fire ants
Or terrified termites, running away
From my echidna tongue, that each day
Digs, and probes, and laps ever deeper.

I have watched new songlines
Form across the Outback of my face,
Frowns and welcome laugh lines,
Tracing patterns, all reflected
In the waterholes of my blue eyes.

Stars freewheeling overhead
Harmonised and helped me remember
What I never knew, and so had not forgotten,
Within my brain, far more neural pathways
Than suns in the night sky. Songlines too.

And sometimes I tracked a dark star.
Looked up, and cast my eyes down to Earth,
Saw strange tracks and patterns in the red soil
That led me astray, confused my singing,
Made me lose my way. Took me from my dreaming.

In those times, warring songlines from other souls
Drowned out my voice and reduced me
At worst to silence, at best to stammering

And stuttering, as if words were my enemies
Sticking in my pricking throat. Painful days.

But just as in a red desert, when sun scrapes life
From Earth's surface, my songs and singing
Burrowed deep, and in time, when enough salt rain
Of painful tears had fallen, springtime sprang again,
And there was still singing somewhere within me.

Poetry matters, not simply as a distraction
From loss, longing or common human yearning,
But for far more. Words ordered in poetic pattern
Take on mythic, ceremonial form, as if in the firelight
We can sit and tell the world's tales around the flames.

And in this moment of pre-dawn blackness,
Outside my West Country cottage window,
I think and link and listen to the new songlines
Blown in, from far distance, on an unseen solar wind,
Or come, bubbling up, from old memories, fermenting.

A new day begins, and endlessness awaits.
Walking across the Outback of my mistakes
And hopes and dreams of schemes yet to come.
Of smiling ancestors' faces dead but never gone,
Accompanying me, in harmony, as I sing my song.

Chronology

1914 Birth of Dylan Thomas at No 5, Cwmdonkin Drive, in Swansea, Wales.

1925 Swansea Grammar School. His father was an English teacher.

1930 Dylan begins the first of his poetry notebooks.

1931 Starts work as a Reporter on the *South Wales Daily Post*.

1932 Leaves the newspaper but continues as a freelance journalist.

1933 'And death shall have no dominion' published in *New English Weekly*

1933 First visit to London.

1934 Dylan moves to London.

1935 His first collection – *18 Poems* – is published.

1936 Dylan moves to Cornwall and meets Caitlin Macamara.

1936 Dylan's second collection – *25 Poems* – is published.

1937 Dylan and Caitlin are married in Penzance, Cornwall.

1937 First BBC Radio Broadcast – *Life and the Modern Poet*

1938 Dylan and Caitlin move into his parent's house.

1938 Dylan and Caitlin move to Laugharne.

1939 Llewelyn is born.

1939 A poetry and prose collection is published, *The Map of Love*.

1939 *The World I Breathe* – first American collection.

1940 Moves to London.

1940 Publication of *Portrait of the Artist As a Young Dog*.

1940 Starts to write propaganda film scripts.

1943 Publication of *New Poems*.

1943 Aeronwy is born in London.

1944 Family moves to Bosham in Sussex.

1944 Family moves to New Quay in Cardiganshire.

1945 Records *Memories of Christmas* for BBC Welsh Service.

1946 'Fern Hill' is published as part of *Deaths and Entrances*.

1946 In America, *Selected Writings* is published.

1949 Dylan and family move, in May, to the Boat House in Laugharne.

1949 Colm is born in Carmarthen.

1950 *26 Poems* delivered to his publisher.

1950 First American reading tour. Three months. Dylan flew by Pan Am. Feb 20th.

1951 'Do Not Go Gentle' published.

1952 Second American tour. January to May, with Caitlin. Arguing over women fans.

1952 Recordings for Caedmon Records.

1952 *Collected Poems 1934-52* published.

1952 Death of Dylan's father at the age of 76.

1953 3rd American tour. May. Six weeks tour. Returned by air.

1953 4th American tour. Against medical advice.

1953 *Under Milk Wood* delivered to the BBC. Performances in New York City.

1953 Dylan's 39th birthday.

1953 During NY reading tour, falls into a coma after doctor's injections. Nov 4th.

1953 Caitlin flies to New York as an emergency. Sat with him, in coma, for four days.

1953 Dylan dies at St Vincent's Hospital. Aged 39.

1953 Over all four American readings tours, Dylan travelled 30,000 miles.

1953 Caitlin returned to Wales by sea with Dylan's coffin.

1953 Dylan buried on November 24ᵗʰ, 1953 at St Martin's Church, Laugharne.

1994 Caitlin Thomas died in Italy (80) on July 31ˢᵗ, after a long illness.

1994 Caitlin Thomas buried in Laugharne, next to Dylan.

2000 Death of Llewelyn Thomas (61).

2009 Death of Aeronwy Thomas-Ellis (66).

2012 Death of Colm Thomas (63).